RETAINING YOUR FOODSERVICE EMPLOYEES

FOODSERVICE EMPLOYEE MANAGEMENT SERIES

Staffing Your Foodservice Operation
Disciplining Your Foodservice Employees

Retaining Your Foodservice Employees

40 WAYS TO BETTER EMPLOYEE RELATIONS

KAREN EICH DRUMMOND

VNR VAN NOSTRAND REINHOLD
New York

Library of Congress Catalog Card Number 91-17673
ISBN 0-442-00571-7

Printed in the United States of America.

Van Nostrand Reinhold
115 Fifth Avenue
New York, New York 10003

Chapman and Hall
2-6 Boundary Row
London, SE1 8HN, England

Thomas Nelson Australia
102 Dodds Street
South Melbourne 3205
Victoria, Australia

Nelson Canada
1120 Birchmount Road
Scarborough, Ontario MIK 5G4, Canada

16 15 14 13 12 11 10 9 8 7 6 5 4 3 2 1

Library of Congress Cataloging-in-Publication Data

Drummond, Karen Eich.
Retaining your foodservice employees : 40 ways to better employee relations / Karen Eich Drummond.
p. cm.
Includes bibliographical references (p.) and index.
ISBN 0-442-00571-7
1. Food service—Personnel management. 2. Labor turnover.
I. Title.
TX911.3.P4D785 1991
647.95'068'3—dc20 91-17673
CIP

To all the foodservice employees who work,
and have worked, with me

CONTENTS

Introduction

Employee turnover of nonmanagement foodservice personnel has long been a major concern to owners and operators. *Turnover* refers to the loss of an employee and the need to find a replacement. Turnover, defined as a percentage, is calculated as follows:

$$\text{Turnover Rate} = \frac{\text{Number of replacements}}{\text{Average number of employees}} \times 100\%$$

In the restaurant business, about half of all separations—such as resignations or terminations—occur within the first 30 days of employment. Turnover rates vary, but many fall between 100 and 150 percent (National Restaurant Association, 1990). In other words, an operator can count on replacing each of his or her current employees at least once during a 12-month period of time.

Turnover can happen either because of voluntary action, such as resignation or retirement, or because of involuntary action, such as termination, lay-off, or discharge when a temporary position ends. When an employee resigns, he or she is basically firing you. Martin Yate, in *Keeping the Best,** describes what happens.

> He is essentially saying: Look; I've examined this long and hard. To be quite frank about it, you just haven't lived up to my expectations: I'm afraid I'm going to have to cut you loose. To go on like this would be a real mistake for both of us, like trying to fit a square peg in a round hole. I know this might hurt a little bit now, but in the long run, I think you'll agree that it's for the best. So OK; I'm gone as of Monday.

That probably sounds a bit like your own "You're fired" speech; but here your employee is telling you.

*Martin Yate, *Keeping the Best,* Holbrook, MA: Bob Adams, Inc., 1991, p. 24.

With employee resignations come certain costs. Hiring an unskilled hourly employee who does not work out may cost between $400 and $1,500, or typically the equivalent of that worker's pay for a month. The figures can increase to $2,000 to $3,000 for skilled employees such as line cooks and servers. This basically covers expenses for recruiting and selecting a new candidate, doing the necessary paperwork for the new hire (such as payroll and benefit records), training, and overtime costs incurred while the position is vacant.

It often takes 5 weeks or more for a vacant position to be filled when one considers recruiting, interviewing, selecting, and giving the new employee time to leave the former job and to be trained on the new job. The cost of filling a position can increase with the length of time the position goes unfilled and the amount of skill and training required. Even worse, high turnover tends to lower employee morale, decrease quality of service, and produce stress for managers. Worst of all unmanaged turnover can cause a significant loss of customers.

The high turnover experienced in the foodservice industry has also become a serious problem because of the difficulty operators have in finding qualified replacements as a result of the shrinking labor pool and competition from other retail industries.

We can no longer treat employees as disposable assets. Employees are the most important resource; without enthusiastic and loyal employees, a company can never achieve excellence. Although some operators still show more loyalty to the bottom right-hand corner of their profit-and-loss statements than to their employees, others have discovered that by taking care of employees, the employees take care of the customers, and sales take care of themselves.

There is a new emphasis on resolving costly turnover and staffing problems by making efforts to retain employees. Managing for retention requires an understanding of what makes employees stay in their jobs, and that is the subject of this book.

Employees today have different needs than they had 20 or 30 years ago. They want to be treated first as individuals, and second as employees. They do not automatically give loyalty and commitment in exchange for their paychecks.

Each chapter of this book discusses a different facet of what today's employees want from their jobs in order to stay and then lists specific actions you can take to satisfy these needs. The first rule of employee retention is to hire the right people; that is the topic of the first book in this series, *Staffing Your Foodservice Operation*. In this book, you will find 40 ways to hold onto your employees. Remember when using these guidelines that each one of your employees is unique and will respond differently to different incentives. For instance, some of your employees may really enjoy being involved in job-related decision making—such involvement makes them want to stay; whereas others appreciate having flexible hours so they can attend college. Remember, also, that taking care of your employees is an investment with multiple returns. In addition to increasing retention rates, taking care of your employees tends to improve service quality and increase productivity, sales, and profits.

40 WAYS TO BETTER EMPLOYEE RELATIONS

1. Write an effective vision statement.
2. Develop guiding principles.
3. Institutionalize your vision and guiding principles.
4. Give a friendly greeting to your employees each day and speak courteously with them.
5. Actively listen to your employees.
6. Give a hand to your employees when appropriate.
7. Do not hover over your employees.
8. Treat employees fairly and consistently.
9. Never discuss an employee's performance with another employee.
10. Keep your employees informed.
11. Involve your employees.
12. When feasible, offer employee counseling and wellness programs.
13. Use up-to-date and accurate job descriptions.
14. Orient new employees.
15. Train employees to do their jobs well.
16. Coach your employees.
17. Formally evaluate employee performance at least once yearly.
18. Set corrective action guidelines and communicate them to employees.
19. Handle counterproductive behaviors using a two-step process.
20. Prevent counterproductive behaviors.
21. Reward your employees.
22. Follow employee reward guidelines.
23. Pay for performance.
24. Institute a profit-sharing or other gain-sharing program for employees.
25. Help employees see the end result of their work.
26. Let your employees make as many of their own decisions as possible.
27. Cross-train employees and rotate their positions.
28. Give employees special assignments.
29. Have a career ladder and promote from within.
30. Offer employees opportunities for personal and professional development.
31. Bring in people from the community for tours and cooking classes.
32. Be able to perform the jobs you supervise.
33. Manage your time.
34. Be visible.
35. Be a good role model.
36. Establish competitive and equitable pay rates.
37. Offer a competitive benefit package suited to your employees.
38. Provide a reasonable work schedule.
39. Provide a pleasant, safe, and clean work environment.
40. Have fun while you work.

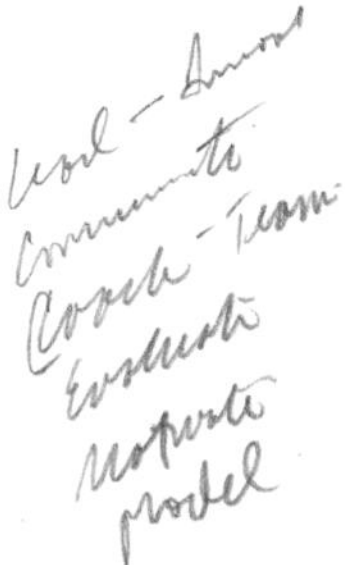

1

Employees Want the Big Picture

1. Write an effective vision statement.
2. Develop guiding principles.
3. Institutionalize your vision and guiding principles.

The establishment of a positive work environment from which employees are hesitant to leave requires a vision, one that shows employees where they are going, why they are going there, and how they will get there. Without it, there is little direction and motivation. Visions are written statements, often called mission statements or credos, that describe an appealing and realistic goal for the company and its employees.

Warren Bennis and Burt Nanus, in their book, *Leaders,** wonderfully describe the benefits of having a vision statement.

> When the organization has a clear sense of its purpose, direction, and desired future state and when this image is widely shared, individuals are able to find their own roles both in the organization and in the larger society of which they are a part. This empowers individuals and confers status upon them because they can see themselves as part of a worthwhile enterprise. They gain a sense of importance, as they are transformed from robots blindly following instructions to human beings engaged in a creative and purposeful venture.

This chapter will address the three steps needed to create and impart a shared company vision.

*Warren Bennis and Burt Nanus, *Leaders,* New York: Harper & Row, 1985 pp. 90–91.

1. Write an Effective Vision Statement

Your company's vision statement should briefly explain

The type of business you are in and why
Your orientation to your guests and employees
Where you are going and what you are working toward

In brief, your vision statement should be a statement of beliefs and intents.

To be effective, the length of the vision statement should range from one to five sentences, so as to enable employees to read it quickly and possibly commit it to memory. The vision statement should also be

Attainable
Clear
Passionate
Easy to relate to
Desirable to work toward

Figure 1-1 is a sample vision statement.

A vision statement is often developed by top management, with middle- and lower-level managers and employees sometimes being asked to participate. Although participatory approaches are more time-consuming, they are more likely to result in a lasting vision because of the increased employee commitment. When top management mandates a vision, the vision is less likely to succeed, especially when there is a discrepancy between the vision and the deep-seated attitudes of the employees. While employees may act supportive, feelings of resentment and resistance are likely to be hiding under the surface. Employees have a greater interest in supporting a vision that they helped to establish than in one they are forced to accept.

Fig. 1-1 VISION STATEMENT

We, the employees of **Your Neighborhood Restaurant,** are in the business of running a family restaurant and providing good food, reasonable prices, and courteous service to our guests. We recognize that in order to maintain profitability, we must continually assess and meet our guests' needs, as well as attract new guests. We are also committed to creating an environment in which every employee is a team member and is encouraged to participate in shaping and achieving our mutual goals.

2. Develop Guiding Principles

The next step is to develop a set of guiding principles for your company based on the vision statement. These principles will spell out in more detail what was mentioned briefly in your vision statement; therefore you must examine what you hold important with regard to your employees, guests, and company direction. For example, you may have a commitment to excellence in guest service or employee development. Following are questions that will help you develop your company's guiding principles, sometimes referred to as your company's philosophy or creed.

EMPLOYEES
Who are your employees? What do you expect from them? Do you want them to be guest-oriented, well trained, team players, involved in decision making, and so on? Conversely, what can your employees expect from you? Can they count on good working conditions, advancement opportunities, and good pay?

GUESTS
Who are your guests? What are their needs? How will you meet their needs?

COMPANY DIRECTION
What do you want your guests to think of when they hear your company's name? Service, excellent food, quick service, a good value? Where do your want your company to be in 5 years?

At this step, employee involvement is vital. A vision cannot be established by decree or coercion. If employees are involved in the development of guiding principles, they will develop a sense of ownership and a commitment to implement them. Through confidential surveys (see Fig. 1-2) or meetings, find out what is important to your employees. Without their involvement, the statement will not be a shared vision.

It is also important at this point to include only those principles that you are able to back up with action. If your employees see that parts of your guiding principles are hogwash, the vision—and the image of your company—loses credibility.

Your guiding principles will probably include some of these important values.

- To build and maintain a positive organizational climate
- To treat employees as the key to your success

Fig. 1-2 EMPLOYEE INPUT SURVEY

EMPLOYEE INPUT SURVEY

Your Neighborhood Restaurant

1. From your point of view, what kind of business are we in? (For example: a service business, the restaurant business, etc.) ____________________

____

____

2. From your perspective, why are we in business? (For example: to make money, to give guests what they want, to provide great food and service, to provide jobs, etc.) ____________________

____

____

3. What do you think is treated as very important in this restaurant? (For example: good food, quick service, friendliness, etc.) ____________________

____

____

4. What are some of the characteristics of our guests? (For example: age, marital status, income, etc.) ____________________

____

5. Is our number of guests growing or shrinking? ____________________

____

6. What do our customers want when they come to our restaurant? (For example: a relaxing environment, good food, friendly service, a change of pace, etc.) How do you know this? (For example: through conversation, intuition, etc.) ____________________

____

____

7. How well do we meet our guests' needs as described in item 6? ________

____

____

8. Do you think that teamwork is stressed?

   ______ Always

   ______ Usually

   ______ Seldom

   ______ Never

Fig. 1-2 Continued

9. Do you think management actively encourages your participation in the shaping and achievement of our goals?

 ______ Always
 ______ Usually
 ______ Seldom
 ______ Never

10. What do you want to get out of your job (besides a paycheck)? Do you think management helps meet these goals?

 ____

 ____

11. What is unique about our restaurant? What do we do well?

 ____

 ____

12. Are there restaurants in the surrounding area that do a better job than we do? What do they do better? (For example: better food, better service, nicer dining room, more relaxed atmosphere, etc.) ______________

 ____

 ____

13. What do you think we should be doing 5 years from now?

 ____

 ____

Fig. 1-3 STATEMENT OF GUIDING PRINCIPLES

GUIDING PRINCIPLES FOR
Your Neighborhood's Restaurant

Our guests and our employees are the key to our success as a profitable family restaurant. We are committed to understanding, anticipating, and responding to each guest's needs with service excellence. For our guests, we also continually strive to provide high quality food at reasonable prices.

For our employees, we think it is vital to provide the needed training and opportunities for personal growth to help each one contribute and grow. We seek and welcome their ideas and opinions.

We expect our employees to learn all they can about their jobs and to take an active role in influencing the decisions affecting their jobs. We also expect them to work as team members and demonstrate professional conduct towards each other and our guests at all times.

- To stay close to and take care of guests
- To offer quality
- To be open to innovation
- To recognize the importance of growth and profits

Figure 1-3 contains a sample statement of guiding principles.

3. Institutionalize Your Vision and Guiding Principles

The preceding steps are easy. To translate words into actions, to institutionalize your vision and guiding principles, is more difficult. Have you ever worked for someone who told you how important employees are to your success, and then, in front of you, criticized an employee for making a mistake? If your company has a wonderful vision statement and guiding principles, but its actions are not consistent with them, your employees pick up on the discrepancy immediately. They become disillusioned and lose respect for management. The vision becomes a bad joke, and employees wonder why they are working for such a poorly run operation.

The following systems within a company can provide excellent ways to implement the vision and guiding principles.

- Quality and service standards
- Job functions and performance evaluation

- Training
- Operational planning
- Annual budgeting
- Organizational structure
- Advertising and promotional literature
- Company publications such as newsletters

Thinking through how beliefs can be reinforced using these systems is essential to success.

In addition, management must consistently model the company's guiding principles and affirm employees who model them. Even before employees are hired, they need to be exposed to the guiding principles—and again during orientation and training. Your guiding principles can be communicated continually through meetings, memos, brochures, conversations, newsletters, speeches, training sessions, posters, and so forth. Repetition helps to make the vision second nature to employees, who, it is hoped, were also involved in the process of developing them.

A method that is helpful in institutionalizing the vision is to shorten the statement to a slogan. For example, McDonalds's slogan is "Quality, Service, Cleanliness," and Marriott Corporation's slogan is "Our business is people serving people." McDonalds's slogan appears in every crew member's handbook and on posters in food preparation areas. Slogans are very effective in helping to institutionalize the vision because they are short, remembered, and remind the employee of what is important, something many employers never communicate.

Another example of a successful slogan is that of a Seattle, Washington, company that operates fine-dining restaurants. "We Always Guarantee Satisfaction" was printed on every menu and guest check. It was then shortened to the acronym WAGS and even developed into a logo. This logo appeared on everything—report forms, training manuals, posters, newsletters, pins, shirts, name tags—even underwear. Each employee also signed a contract stating that he or she would follow through in putting the slogan into practice. In this manner, the vision was successfully institutionalized.

2

Employees Want to Work for a Manager Who Respects, Trusts, and Cares About Them

4. Give a friendly greeting to your employees each day and speak courteously with them.
5. Actively listen to your employees.
6. Give a hand to your employees when appropriate.
7. Do not hover over your employees.
8. Treat employees fairly and consistently.
9. Never discuss an employee's performance with another employee.
10. Keep your employees informed.
11. Involve your employees.
12. When feasible, offer employee counseling and wellness programs.

Showing a lack of respect and trust for your employees is one of the quickest ways to lose them. When employees feel they are being taken advantage of, not listened to, treated like children, ignored, or belittled in front of their peers, they do not stay. Respect, trust, and caring are the foundations for all relationships—personal or professional. Without them, any working relationship suffers and gradually disintegrates.

When you treat your employees with respect and trust, they are likely to return that respect and trust. Use the Golden Rule of Management: treat your employees the way you would want to be treated. Trust each employee until he or she proves you wrong. If you take care of your employees, your employees will take care of your customers, and sales will take care of themselves.

4. Give a Friendly Greeting to Your Employees Each Day and Speak Courteously with Them

The simplest way to show respect and caring is to give a warm, sincere greeting to your employees each day as you walk through their work areas. Ask each person how he or she is doing and chat for a few minutes. If an employee told you a few days ago that one of his children was sick, ask how the child is doing. If an employee was recently given a raise, check to see that the raise was included in last week's paycheck.

Always be courteous to your employees. Sometimes managers make the mistake of talking to their people from a position of power or status and they command their employees around the kitchen. There's no place in a busy foodservice operation for egos and employees will simply not put up with it. Talk to your employees the way you want your own boss to talk to you, that is, with respect and courtesy. Request, do not demand, employees to do things, and be sure to say please and thank you.

5. Actively Listen to Your Employees

Would any of your employees make one of the following comments about you to a co-worker when you are not around?

"I am never sure if what I am saying gets through."
"Why bother talking to the boss? He only hears what he wants to hear."
"It's hard to get a word in edgewise."
"The boss interrupts me constantly."
"The boss barely looks at me when I talk to her."
"Between his phone and the secretary, it's hard to get his attention for more than 5 minutes at a time."
"The boss always puts off talking to me."
"The boss acts as if she knows it all, and I doubt she hears a word I say."

Poor listening impacts tremendously on our ability to retain employees. Just think of the situations in which listening is required: training, coaching, and scheduling work, to name just a few.

Listening is probably the most important, yet the most poorly performed, part of communication. How often, in a conversation with an employee, are we concentrating on our own response when we really should be listening for the employee's message? The untrained listener typically understands and retains about 50 percent of a conversation, and only 25 percent of it 2 days later. Little wonder employees complain that we do not hear them, and that tension and distrust result.

Our poor listening habits result quite often from the fact that we think much more quickly than we talk. You can talk to someone at 100 to 150 words per minute but you can think, or talk to yourself, at 250 to 500 words per minute. When you are listening to someone, it is therefore very easy to fill in this difference in speed with your own thoughts (such as your response) and before you know it, you are not hearing very much. Another obstacle to listening includes a distracting environment, such as the production areas, which are too noisy and lack privacy.

On the other hand, when we effectively listen to our employees, we build understanding, trust, and morale. Listening shows genuine respect for your employees' judgment and intelligence. When employees feel listened to, they are more likely to say something like "I like my boss. I can talk to him and he understands what I am trying to say." Even when we cannot come through with what an employee is asking for, if the employee feels that we listened and understood, he or she is less likely to be upset or angry. Another benefit of listening to your employees is that they will be more likely to listen to you as well.

Active listening is the most effective level of listening, and it requires putting yourself into your employee's shoes. It does not come naturally; rather, active listening is a learned skill requiring much concentration and sensitivity. Instead of hearing what you want to hear, you have to work on understanding the employee's message. You need to listen not only to the employee's verbal message, but also to *how* it is being said and what is *not* being said. The active listener does not interrupt the employee, but skillfully uses questions to gain understanding.

The active listener has three important skills, referred to as attending, sensing, and responding skills.

1. The active listener uses attending skills, which include giving both appropriate verbal and nonverbal messages to indicate attentiveness. Examples of attending behaviors include making eye contact, nodding the head, or using expressions such as "Go on," and creating a private atmosphere in which to talk.
2. The active listener uses sensing skills to examine the nonverbal

behaviors or messages of the speaker. Nonverbal communication includes thoughts and ideas that an individual communicates, not only through the voice, but also through the body, physical distance, or dress. The active listener attends to body language—specifically to body posture, facial expressions, vocal inflections, and gestures that are used to communicate attitudes and feelings.

3. Responding skills are used by the active listener to understand the speaker's message to the fullest. These include asking questions to get more information or clarify feelings, trying to get the speaker to say more, or helping the speaker toward greater understanding.

Guidelines for Actively Listening to Your Employees

- As much as possible, try to speak privately with an employee in an environment conducive to listening and free from distractions such as telephone calls and other interruptions.
- Whether the conversation is one concerning discipline, evaluation of performance, or most other topics, it is best to state the purpose of the meeting and then let the employee tell his or her own story first.
- The most basic guideline for active listening is that it is impossible to listen and talk at the same time. In other words, be quiet! You cannot be listening very well if you are interrupting the employee to get across your thoughts. So keep quiet, relax, and listen to the speaker until it is an appropriate time to speak.
- Show the employee you are trying to listen by maintaining good eye contact, leaning slightly forward, nodding your head affirmatively, using verbal expressions such as "Yes" or "Go on" to show interest, and standing or sitting close to the employee without violating his or her personal space. Be relaxed. Smile.
- Concentrate your attention on what the employee is saying as well as his or her feelings, emotions, and intentions. Train yourself to focus on the words, feelings, and intent of the employee. Ignore distractions such as kitchen noises.
- Listen for the employee's main ideas—specific concerns or needs—which may or may not be obvious from the conversation. Ask yourself, "Do I know for certain what he (she) means?" Listen for unspoken meanings behind the words.
- React to ideas, not to the employee. Always support the self-respect and self-esteem of the employee.
- Do not jump to conclusions or make snap judgments. Suspend judgment and listen objectively.

- Keep your emotions in line. Emotions, particularly anger, limit your ability to listen.
- Try to understand what the employee is saying from his or her point of view. You might find that what the employee is saying is worth considering, even though you did not think so at first.
- Do not close your mind to information that is new, hard to understand, or complex.
- Do not discount an entire message because of disagreement with one point.
- Encourage the employee to tell you more by making statements such as "Tell me about it," "Let's discuss it," or "I am interested in what you have to say."
- Table 2-1 explains how, with examples, to ask various types of questions to enhance understanding.
- When listening to an employee and you cannot give an immediate answer, be sure to reply as soon as possible. This is crucial, as otherwise the employee will feel forgotten, left out, or unimportant.

6. Give a Hand to Your Employees When Appropriate

When things are hectic and your employees are overloaded, lend a hand. This is really appreciated and lets your employees know you care. Although you do not want to do this on a daily basis (because employees may start to depend on you), it is an appropriate gesture in emergencies, such as when the dishwasher breaks down.

7. Do Not Hover Over Your Employees

When you hover over your employees, they sense that you do not trust them and feel they are being treated like children. By checking in with them from time to time, you send a message of trust that will, in most cases, be reciprocated. When monitoring employees, do it from the perspective of checking to see if there are any problems you might help to resolve. If you use this approach, employees will see your visits as helpful and caring.

8. Treat Employees Fairly and Consistently

Fairness means being objective and impartial in your dealings with employees, such as in employee evaluations, coaching, and corrective actions. Being consistent means treating everyone in the same man-

Table 2-1 Types of Questions to Enhance Understanding

Objective	*Method*	*Listener*
I. Clarifying Check 1. When you want to clarify, want facts, want to explore further, or to check assumptive meaning and understand.	State a what, how, or when question. Then restate what you thought you heard.	1. "Is this the problem as you see it?" 2. "Will you clarify what you mean by . . . ?" 3. "What specifically do you mean by . . . ?" 4. "What I understand you to say is. . . . Is that right?"
II. Accuracy Check 1. To check your listening accuracy, encourage further discussion. 2. To let the person know you grasp the facts.	Restate the person's basic ideas, emphasizing the facts.	1. "As I understand it, the problem is . . . (restatement) Am I hearing you correctly?" 2. "What I think you said was . . ."
III. Feeling Check 1. To show you are listening and understanding. 2. To reduce anxiety, anger, or other negative feelings. 3. To let the person know you understand how he or she feels.	Reflect the person's feelings. Paraphase in your own words what the talker said. Match the talker's depth of meaning, light or serious. Ensure accurate communication of feelings by matching the talker's meaning.	1. "You feel that you didn't get the proper treatment." 2. "It was unjust as you perceived it." 3. "It's annoying to have this happen to you." 4. "It seems to me that you got turned off when your boss talked to you in that angry manner." 5. "I sense that you like doing the job but are not sure how to go about it."

Table 2-1 Continued

Objective	*Method*	*Listener*
IV. Summarizing Check		
1. To focus the discussion and to lead to a new level of discussion. 2. To focus on main points, to offer a springboard for further consideration. 3. To pull important ideas or facts together. 4. To review progress.	Restate, reflect, and summarize major ideas and feelings.	1. "These are the key elements of the problem." 2. "Let's see now, we've examined these factors." 3. "These seem to be the key ideas you express." 4. "To summarize, the main points as I heard them are . . ."
V. Noncommittal Acknowledgment		
1. To stay neutral and show you are interested. 2. To encourage; to keep a person talking.	Don't agree or disagree. Use noncommittal words with a positive tone of voice. Noncommittal acknowledgement.	1. "I see . . ." 2. "Uh-huh . . ." 3. "Mm-hmm . . ." 4. I get the idea . . ." "I understand." Silence during the pause.
VI. Acknowledgment		
Acknowledge the problem.	State that there is a problem.	1. "Tell me about it." 2. "That does seem to present a problem."

Listening: The Forgotten Skill, Madelyn Burley-Allen. Copyright © 1982 by Madelyn Burley-Allen. Reprinted by permission of John Wiley & Sons, Inc.

ner and applying all rules and procedures equally. Lack of fairness and consistency is among the most frequent complaints by employees against management. For instance, Sam, a cook, asks for next Friday night off and his request is denied. Two days later he hears that his boss has just allowed another cook, who is very friendly with the general manager, to take Friday night off. Sam is upset and thinks about calling in sick on Friday.

This type of problem occurs all too frequently in the foodservice industry, and it has a strong impact on employees. Managers need to function as a team and interpret policies and procedures fairly and consistently for all employees.

9. Never Discuss an Employee's Performance with Another Employee

To maintain the respect and trust of each of your employees, do not discuss an employee's performance (or anything else for that matter) with another employee. This information is strictly confidential. During performance evaluations and interviews regarding disciplinary actions, employees often try to bring up other employees' behavior in the discussion. When this happens, make a statement such as, "Right now we are discussing your performance only. I am sure you would not want me to discuss your performance with another employee, so please do not ask me to do that to someone else."

10. Keep Your Employees Informed

Lack of information about what is going on in a company leads employees to become distrustful, indifferent, and unresponsive. It also causes much miscommunication and the spread of misinformation, better known as rumors. When information is supplied by management, employees feel respected, empowered, better able to do their jobs, and they are more receptive to being involved. At the same time, information attracts information, and managers who give out information receive information in return.

There are many ways to keep your employees informed:

Regular meetings, such as weekly cooks' meetings or daily premeal meetings, keep everyone informed about day-to-day operations.

Just walking around the work areas each day, making sure to speak to employees, is another way to keep them informed.

Periodically, have a "State of the Foodservice" meeting and invite all employees. Discuss new developments, anticipated changes, level of business, financial situation, new employees hired, and so on. Take the opportunity to restate the vision and guiding principles of the operation.

Special notices can convey information—posted on bulletin boards, sent to employees' homes, or included in pay envelopes.

Company newsletters, although time-consuming, keep employees informed, as well as reinforce the vision and guiding principles of your company. A newsletter is also a great avenue for employee recognition (Fig. 2-1).

Regular meetings with your employees can be a very useful means to keep employees informed. Unfortunately, if meetings are handled poorly, they can be frustrating and time-consuming. Here are some specific suggestions to make your meetings work better.

Guidelines for Successful Employee Meetings

- Announce meetings well in advance of when they will take place.
- Plan what will be discussed at the meeting and write up an agenda. Post or hand out this agenda in advance so employees have an idea of what will be taking place.
- Set ground rules for meetings such as one person talks at a time, everyone should raise his/her hand to get permission to speak, and everyone must be respectful at all times.
- Start your meeting on time. Do not wait for employees who are late. If you get the meeting going on time, they will get the message to be on time for the next one.
- Use your agenda during the meeting to keep the discussion focused and finish the meeting on time.
- If you want your employees to help solve problems and give their input, limit the meeting to 15 people. Larger groups are fine if you simply need to get information across, but they hinder good discussions.
- Encourage an open flow of ideas by making positive, reinforcing statements about employee ideas. Also, actively listen to your employees and monitor, rather then dominate, the discussion.
- Make sure all viewpoints have a fair hearing.
- When an employee is talking too much and trying to dominate the group, move closer to him or her, and say, "Thank you very much for speaking. I think it's time we hear from someone else." You may also want to appoint this person to take notes of the meeting for you.
- When two employees seem to disagree on something, state the difference of opinion and try to find some common ground.
- Summarize what has been stated and/or decided upon at the meeting.

Fig. 2-1 COMPANY NEWSLETTER

WOOD

Count on me

Winter/Spring, 1991

Heartland Selections

The best reason ever for "eating healthy"

Get ready - we'll soon be launching *Heartland Selections*. Our newest signature program, dedicated to the health and well being of our customers, proves that healthy eating doesn't have to be "twigs and berries". By choosing *Heartland Selections*, our customers will be able to *eat hearty and eat healthy*.

The Wellness committee has been working hard to develop and fine tune this program. Four subcommittees were formed to develop the program's nutritional guidelines, marketing concepts and materials, recipes and training support.

Nutrient Guidelines

To define what our *Heartland Selections* offer, the nutrition subcommittee established criteria that must be strictly adhered to in every recipe. The committee studied guidelines established by the USDA, the American Heart Association, the National Academy of Sciences, and the Cholesterol Education Project to help determine the appropriate content for healthy menu items. Each *Heartland* soup, entree, side dish or dessert portion will have limited amounts of sodium, cholesterol, fat and calories.

Heartland SELECTIONS

A Heartland Selections stir-fried shrimp entree

Marketing

The marketing subcommittee surveyed managers, members of the wellness committee and some of our company chefs to find out what our customers would look for in a wellness program. We determined that the most important concepts to be communicated in our program name and marketing materials are "healthy" and "fresh." Thus, *Heartland Selections* was born. Our name, logo and even the colors chosen symbolize good health, freshness and wholesomeness.

Marketing and merchandising materials will be an important part of our wellness program. They will introduce the program, help us in our consumer education efforts and identify *Heartland Selections* on menus and at point of purchase.

Recipe Development

To be sure our *Heartland Selections* are "on target," the recipe subcommittee asked food service directors what they wanted. All of the recipes submitted have been evaluated for taste, nutritional guidelines, variety, ease of production and readily available ingredients. We also looked for recipes that are contemporary and have good eye appeal. Production procedures are in accordance with HACCP sanitation standards, and recipes are printed for various portion sizes. With our wellness program, we are making a commitment to the health of our customers, so all *Heartland* recipes specify, ***No substitutions permitted.***

(continued next page)

WE ARE PEOPLE PROUD

Cover page of "Count on Me" newsletter, The Wood Company, Winter/Spring, 1991.

Following are general guidelines for informing employees.

Guidelines for Informing Employees

- Be specific and keep the message simple.
- Be knowledgeable. Know what you are talking about.
- Timing is important. Announcing a major change 2 days before it occurs is not timely; it is downright late. Information is best communicated at a time when things are not too hectic.
- Tell employees everything you can without jeopardizing confidentiality.
- Whenever possible, inform employees in person rather than by written communication.
- Include all involved personnel at meetings.
- When informally sharing information with certain groups of employees, make sure you do not leave anyone out.
- Make it a point to give an update to employees who missed a meeting or other informational gathering. This may be accomplished through conversation or by posting minutes of the meeting.
- Sincerely ask for employees' reactions and questions and, of course, listen attentively.

11. Involve Your Employees

Employees who are asked to influence what happens at work tend to develop a sense of ownership, and this feeling of ownership breeds commitment. Involving employees empowers them and demonstrates your respect and trust in them.

Employees can become effectively involved in many managerial activities, such as planning operational changes. They can also be useful in any of the following functions:

Providing information and data
Evaluating work methods
Identifying problems
Proposing suggestions, solutions, or improvements
Deciding on a course of action
Implementing and evaluating a course of action

Employees can tell you better than anyone else how their own jobs should be done—they are the people who do these jobs day in and day out.

Before discussing methods to gain employee input and feedback, let's take a look at some hurdles you will need to clear before anything can happen. First, many employees will feel uncomfortable about giving you feedback. Perhaps in the past they were criticized, given the worst possible jobs to do, or even disciplined, for speaking up. Or perhaps they gave feedback that was always ignored. In any case, there was nothing to be gained by saying anything, so many of your employees are likely to keep their mouths shut.

Second, employees tend to give feedback in different ways. Some employees will tell you what is on their minds any time, any place, in front of others, or alone. Other employees prefer to be less direct and are comfortable only when speaking privately with you. Other employees will never give you any input.

Third, when you ask for employee input at meetings, frequently one or more employees will monopolize the meeting, which makes it very difficult to get feedback from anyone else.

So what can you do to get over these hurdles? Try the following.

- Be genuinely interested in listening to your employees.
- Continually work on developing and maintaining a trusting relationship with your employees. The guidelines in this chapter, as well as guideline 35 (be a good role model), can help in this area.
- Tell your employees on a regular basis that you want to hear from them and that their input is always welcome whether it is good news or bad news. Explain that you will respond to each employee who gives feedback and that there will be absolutely no reprisals. Also explain that such employee input can benefit many different people.
- Be sensitive to your employees' different communication styles. You may need to speak to your quiet employees one-on-one in a private environment to get their feedback.
- To get feedback from as many employees as possible at a meeting, try this technique. Have a meeting with them and state the topic or problem about which you would like their feedback. Explain that you want each person to think about the topic and come up with his or her own ideas to be discussed at the next meeting. When they meet for the second time, ask for all members to give their ideas using a round-robin format, one employee at a time. Only after all employees have expressed their ideas will there be any discussion. Make clear to everyone that no idea is to be ridiculed during the discussion and that everyone is invited to contribute on an equal basis regardless of rank.
- When employees take the time to give you feedback on a topic of mutual concern, they are also taking a chance that you may not

like what they are going to tell you. For this reason, always express your sincere appreciation to your employees for talking to you, even if you do not agree with what they are saying. Also, always respond to what they have told you. If an employee makes a request you cannot honor, explain why in detail. Do not just say, "Oh, it's not in the budget."

There are various methods to obtain employee input and feedback, ranging from the traditional suggestion box to employee involvement at management meetings. Here are some examples.

- The simplest way to get employees involved is to talk to them frequently on the job. Ask them for their opinions and advice on pertinent topics. It is amazing how much more they will share at *their* work station than in *your* office.
- Probably one of the most popular ways to involve employees is through planned problem-solving meetings between management and employees. For example, one small restaurant chain has monthly meetings for upper management and employees to discuss problems and suggestions. Each restaurant elects and sends two servers, two cooks, and one bartender to attend these meetings. In another foodservice, managers and employees meet daily to exchange ideas and discuss operational issues. Employees are asked for input into operational decisions, such as portion control, and these issues are discussed using a consensus decision-making philosophy. In this method, there is no consensus or action taken until each person involved feels at least 70 percent sure about a certain plan of action. Once consensus is reached, each person is expected to give 100 percent support to the decision.
- Have a "talk back to the boss" program. Periodically invite your employees to meet and discuss their concerns. This type of program has been used by Domino's, the pizza chain, to solicit ideas by mail from 40,000 employees in its "If you were the boss" campaign. The objective was to gain valuable input.
- Implement a suggestion program in which employees are asked to write down or otherwise express any suggestions they have to improve work methods or any aspect of their jobs. A response rate in a suggestion program is typically about 15 percent, of which about one-quarter of the responses are implemented. Suggestion programs often center on topics such as how to save money in a certain area or how to reduce accidents, and may include a financial or other reward to employees whose suggestions are implemented. When starting a suggestion program, be sure you have time to review the suggestions and to give each employee feedback

on his or her suggestion. The ideas employees submit may sometimes not be wonderful or important, but your employees are. Be sure to give sufficient credit where it is due.

- Instead of a suggestion box, and depending on your purpose, you may want to implement a communication box. Employees are encouraged to submit not only suggestions, but also questions, concerns, and comments to the communication box. Again, it is important to respond to all communications so that employees see that their efforts are worthwhile.

Involving employees is particularly crucial for implementing change successfully. Ask employees to participate to the furthest extent possible in the decision about how the change will be made. This stimulates employees to discuss, make suggestions, and think positively about the change, discourages resistance, and encourages employee commitment to the change rather than mere compliance. Employees should also be involved in developing a final plan detailing exactly how the change will occur, including who does what, when, where, and how.

12. When Feasible, Offer Employee Counseling and Wellness Programs

Counseling programs, usually called employee assistance programs (EAPs), are an expansion of traditional occupational alcoholism programs, which began 40 years ago. About one-third of the U.S. work force has access to EAPs according to the Association of Labor-Management Administrators and Consultants on Alcoholism, based in Arlington, Virginia, which represents about 6,000 EAP practitioners. Larger companies are more likely to have EAPs than smaller companies. Organizations such as Marriott, Kentucky Fried Chicken, and Lettuce Entertain You offer counseling and referral services to some or all of their employees.

EAPs function to help troubled employees in personal crises, as well as those with emotional or substance abuse problems. At a time when the hospitality industry needs to retain employees, EAPs can help to get employees back on their feet and back to work.

An operator may hire its own counselor to administer a program, employ an outside counselor under contract to the EAP, or use a counselor affiliated with a nonprofit social services group. Outside counselors estimate that EAPs cost the employer from $.75 to $3 per employee per month. The price varies according to the number of services provided. Although the scope of services varies from company to company, most include initial consultation to determine the nature and extent of the problem and counseling targeted at easing or resolving it.

When starting an EAP, a company should have a written policy statement to explain its objectives for the program. The statement should include the fact that the EAP is strictly confidential. This information and instructions about how to use the program should be explained clearly to all employees. In addition, managers and supervisors need to be trained to know how and when to make referrals; if an employee is having personal problems that are affecting job performance, the EAP program should be suggested as a source of help. Referrals are also appropriate if an employee appears to be chronically angry, confused, depressed, or withdrawn.

Guidelines for Referring an Employee to an EAP Program

- Do emphasize confidentiality.
- Do explain that going for help does not exclude the employee from disciplinary procedures nor does it include special privileges.
- Do stick to discussing job performance and explain in very specific terms what the employee needs to do in order to perform according to expectations.
- Do give the employee the appropriate information in writing on how to contact an EAP counselor.
- Do not try to diagnose the employee's problem and do not ask why the employee is performing in a certain way. This only leads to excuse making.
- Do not discuss in depth the employee's personal problems with him or her. Do not become the employee's counselor.
- Do not take responsibility for solving the employee's problems.
- Do not be swayed by emotional pleas, tactics to gain sympathy, or hard luck stories.

Successful EAP programs share the following characteristics:

1. The program is accessible 24 hours a day, 7 days a week.
2. Employees are given the phone number of the EAP office.
3. The program is carried out by qualified professionals who are understanding of personal problems.
4. Involvement of the family is encouraged when it is relevant to treatment.
5. The program is advertised and available to the employee's entire family.

6. Confidentiality is strictly maintained.
7. The employee does not receive any special favors or exemptions from on-the-job rules during treatment.
8. Managers are given training on how and when to make referrals.

Promoting good health in the workplace with what are commonly called *wellness programs* has been growing in popularity. Major components of health promotion and disease prevention programs include physical fitness, detection and reduction of the risks of hypertension and heart disease, general nutrition, weight control, elimination of smoking, and stress management. Such programs are usually provided by the employer at minimal or no cost to the employee.

A wellness program has the potential to reduce use of health services, lower health-care costs, increase productivity, reduce absenteeism, lower turnover, improve employee morale, and increase knowledge of health risks. It can also contribute to a positive company image and become a valued benefit for employees.

Wellness programs may include exercise classes, seminars and workshops on such topics as stress management and smoking cessation, and hypertension and cholesterol screenings. At a modest level, you can promote health awareness among employees through printed materials such as pamphlets and posters. At the next level, you might invite health professionals to speak at workshops and seminars. At the highest level, you might provide programs in which employees actively participate.

Some companies, such as General Mills, promote a healthful employee life-style through awareness, education, and participation. The program, called Framework, incorporates a multidisciplinary approach that includes physical fitness, nutrition, mental health, chemical dependency counseling, first aid training in cardiopulmonary resuscitation, safety awareness, and recreation. Information about these subjects is presented in seminars, displays, and publications. This material is reinforced by employee participation and one-on-one consultation as the employee desires. The Framework program encourages employees to take responsibility for a positive life-style, both at work and at home.

Other companies, such as McGuffey's Restaurants (Asheville, North Carolina), have started health awareness programs for their corporate managers and general managers. They will eventually include all managers and hourly employees. The programs include a health risk appraisal, such as depicted in Fig. 2-2, and physical fitness tests. Employees set goals based on the results.

Occasionally, costs or the smallness of an employee population may appear as a barrier to offering wellness activities; however, emerging wellness councils may offer the required assistance. Wellness councils consist of businesses within a certain locality that have joined to share health expertise and resources in an effort to expand the availability of health promotion programs to employees. Wellness councils are being formed in cities across the country with the assistance of the Health Insurance Association of America. The wellness council movement is growing quickly.

Small businesses will find that many local voluntary health agencies, hospitals, chambers of commerce, cooperative extension offices, public health departments, and colleges and universities may be able to assist them in their wellness efforts. An alternative is to ask employees to share program costs or to provide partial reimbursement for employees joining programs available in the community. Appendix A contains a list of resources for developing a wellness program.

Fig. 2-2 HEALTH RISK APPRAISAL

HEALTH STYLE—A SELF-TEST

A Test for Better Health

If you never smoke, enter a score of 10 for this section and go to the next section on *Alcohol and Drugs*.

	Almost Always	Sometimes	Almost Never
1. I avoid smoking cigarettes.	2	1	0
2. I smoke only low tar and nicotine cigarettes *or* I smoke a pipe or cigars.	2	1	0

Smoking Score: ________

	Almost Always	Sometimes	Almost Never
1. I avoid drinking alcoholic beverages *or* I drink no more than 1 or 2 drinks a day.	4	1	0
2. I avoid using alcohol or other drugs (especially illegal drugs) as a way of handling stressful situations or the problems in my life.	2	1	0
3. I am careful not to drink alcohol when taking certain medicines (for example, medicine for sleeping, pain, colds, and allergies).	2	1	0
4. I read and follow the label directions when using prescribed and over-the-counter drugs.	2	1	0

Alcohol and Drugs Score: ________

Eating Habits

	Almost Always	Sometimes	Almost Never
1. I eat a variety of foods each day, such as fruits and vegetables, whole grain breads and cereals, lean meats, dairy products, dry peas and beans, and nuts and seeds.	4	1	0
2. I limit the amount of fat, saturated fat, and cholesterol I eat (including fat on meats, eggs, butter, cream, shortenings, and organ meats such as liver).	2	1	0
3. I limit the amount of salt I eat by cooking with only small amounts, not adding salt at the table, and avoiding salty snacks.	2	1	0
4. I avoid eating too much sugar (especially frequent snacks of sticky candy or soft drinks).	2	1	0

Eating Habits Score: ________

Exercise Fitness

	Almost Always	Sometimes	Almost Never
1. I maintain a desired weight, avoiding overweight and underweight.	3	1	0
2. I do vigorous exercises for 15-30 minutes at least 3 times a week (examples include running, swimming, brisk walking).	3	1	0
3. I do exercises that enhance my muscle tone for 15-30 minutes at least 3 times a week (examples include yoga and calisthenics).	2	1	0
4. I use part of my leisure time participating in individual, family, or team activities that increase my level of fitness (such as gardening, bowling, golf, and baseball).	2	1	0

Exercise/Fitness Score: ________

Fig. 2-2 Continued

Stress Control

	Almost Always	Sometimes	Almost Never
1. I have a job or do other work that I enjoy.	2	1	0
2. I find it easy to relax and express my feelings freely.	2	1	0
3. I recognize early, and prepare for, events or situations likely to be stressful for me.	2	1	0
4. I have close friends, relatives, or others whom I can talk to about personal matters and call on for help when needed.	2	1	0
5. I participate in group activities (such as church and community organizations) or hobbies that I enjoy.	2	1	0

Stress Control Score: ________

Safety

	Almost Always	Sometimes	Almost Never
1. I wear a seat belt while riding in a car.	2	1	0
2. I avoid driving while under the influence of alcohol and other drugs.	2	1	0
3. I obey traffic rules and the speed limit when driving.	2	1	0
4. I am careful when using potentially harmful products or substances (such as household cleaners, poisons, and electrical devices).	2	1	0
5. I avoid smoking in bed.	2	1	0

Safety Score: ________

What Scores Mean to YOU

Scores of 9 and 10

Excellent! Your answers show that you are aware of the importance of this area to your health. More importantly, you are putting your knowledge to work for you by practicing good health habits. As long as you continue to do so, this area should not pose a serious health risk. It's likely that you are setting an example for your family and friends to follow. Since you got a very high score on this part of the test, you may want to consider other areas where your scores indicate room for improvement.

Your health practices in this area are good, but there is room for improvement. Look again at the items you answered with a "Sometimes" or "Almost Never". What changes can you make to improve your score? Even a small change can often help you achieve better health.

Your health risks are showing! Would you like more information about the risks you are facing and about why it is important for you to change these behaviors. Perhaps you need help in deciding how to successfully make the changes you desire. In either case, help is available. See the last page of this booklet.

Scores of 0 to 2

Obviously, you were concerned enough about your health to take the test, but your answers show that you may be taking serious and unnecessary risks with your health. Perhaps you are not aware of the risks and what to do about them. You can easily get the information and help you need to improve, if you wish. A source of contact appears on the last page. The next step is up to you.

ASSESSMENT OF RESPECTING, TRUSTING, AND CARING SKILLS

Directions: In the blank space at the front of each item, put the number which best indicates your estimation of the frequency of each behavior.

Scale: 5—Never, 4—Seldom, 3—Occasionally, 2—Usually, 1—Always

_____ 4. Give a friendly greeting to your employees each day and speak courteously with them.

_____ 5. Actively listen to your employees.

_____ 6. Give a hand to your employees when appropriate.

_____ 7. Stay close enough to your employees to know what is going on without hovering over them.

_____ 8. Treat employees fairly and consistently.

_____ 9. Keep employee information confidential.

_____ 10. Keep your employees informed.

_____ 11. Involve your employees.

_____ 12. When feasible, offer employee counseling and wellness programs.

The more frequently you use the above behaviors, the more you show respect, trust, and caring for your employees. In any case where you gave yourself a "3" or higher, use the following checklist to work harder on these skills.

RESPECTING, TRUSTING, AND CARING SKILLS CHECKLIST

Directions: Use this checklist at periodic intervals, such as every month, to see how well you are doing in the selected skill areas. Check off the skills you used, as a way to reinforce your positive behaviors, and circle those skills you have not used but wish to. Keep this checklist handy as a reminder of the skills you want to work on.

4. Give a friendly greeting to your employees each day and speak courteously with them.

   DID YOU:

   _____ Give a warm, sincere greeting to each of your employees each day you worked?
   _____ Chat for a few minutes with some of your employees?
   _____ Speak with your employees the way you would want them to speak to you?
   _____ Request, not demand, employees to do things?

5. Actively listen to your employees.

   DID YOU:

   _____ Speak with employees in an environment as free of distractions as possible?
   _____ Let employees tell their own story first?
   _____ Keep quiet and listen to the speaker without interrupting?
   _____ Show you were trying to listen by maintaining good eye contact, leaning slightly forward, nodding your head, using verbal expressions, and being close to the employee?
   _____ Concentrate your attention on the employee's words, feelings, emotions, and intentions?
   _____ Listen to the employee's main ideas and unspoken meanings?
   _____ React to ideas, not to the employee?
   _____ Listen objectively and not jump to conclusions?
   _____ Keep your emotions in line?
   _____ Try to understand what the employee was saying from his or her point of view?

RESPECTING, TRUSTING AND CARING SKILLS CHECKLIST Continued

_____ Keep your mind open to information even if it was new, hard to understand, or complex?
_____ Not discount the entire message just because you disagreed with one point?
_____ Encourage the employee to tell you more?
_____ Ask questions to clarify and check on understanding?
_____ Get back to the employee with an answer?

6. Give a hand to your employees when appropriate.

DID YOU:

_____ Jump in and help your employees in an emergency?

7. Stay close enough to your employees to know what is going on without hovering over them.

DID YOU:

_____ Check in with employees from time to time?

8. Treat employees fairly and consistently.

DID YOU:

_____ Check that any disciplinary actions taken were fair and consistent with department practice as well as past practice?
_____ Give time off fairly and consistently according to procedures?
_____ Evaluate and coach employee performance impartially?
_____ Avoid granting any of your employees special favors, such as a longer break, just because you like them?

9. Keep employee information confidential.

DID YOU:

_____ Keep all employee information confidential?

10. Keep your employees informed.

DID YOU:

_____ Keep the message simple and specific?

RESPECTING, TRUSTING AND CARING SKILLS CHECKLIST Continued

_____ Keep your employees informed using meetings, notices, etc.?
_____ Have a regularly scheduled meeting(s) with your employees?
_____ Include all involved personnel at meetings?
_____ Announce the meeting in advance?
_____ Set ground rules for your meeting and announce them?
_____ Have an agenda for the meeting and announce it?
_____ Start and end the meeting on time?
_____ Use your agenda to keep the meeting focused?
_____ Keep the meeting group small if you want them to help problem solve?
_____ Encourage an open flow of ideas by making positive, reinforcing statements about employee ideas?
_____ Monitor, rather than dominate, the discussion?
_____ Make sure all viewpoints had a fair hearing?
_____ Ask for feedback from many employees?
_____ Mediate differences of opinion?
_____ Summarize the decisions of the group?
_____ Post meeting minutes?

11. Involve your employees.

DID YOU:

_____ Specifically invite employee involvement on one or more topics?
_____ Talk frequently to your employees at their work station?
_____ Tell employees that you want their input?
_____ Actively listen to someone who gave you input?
_____ Say "thank-you" and give an answer to every employee who gave you feedback?
_____ Make an effort to solicit feedback from quiet employees?

12. When feasible, offer employee counseling and wellness programs.

IF EMPLOYEE COUNSELING OR WELLNESS PROGRAMS ARE AVAILABLE, DID YOU:

_____ Refer a troubled employee to a counselor according to procedure?
_____ Suggest an employee try out the wellness program?

3

Employees Want Clearly Communicated Performance Expectations That Are Supported by Management

13. Use up-to-date and accurate job descriptions.
14. Orient new employees.
15. Train employees to do their jobs well.
16. Coach your employees.
17. Formally evaluate employee performance at least once yearly.
18. Set corrective action guidelines and communicate them to employees.
19. Handle counterproductive behaviors using a two-step process.
20. Prevent counterproductive behaviors.

Employees do not like to fail. If they cannot perform some aspect of their job, they will, if they can, avoid it. When an employee performs poorly, we often jump to the conclusion that the fault lies with the employee. Yet in various studies it has been shown that when an employee does a poor job, it is more likely to be management's fault than the employee's fault. Following are three major reasons that employees perform poorly.

- Employees do not know what they are supposed to do.
- Employees do not know how to do the task.
- Employees do not know why they should do the task.

In each of these cases, poor performance is much more likely to be management's fault than the employee's.

If you want employees to be committed and stay with you, you need to

Communicate all performance expectations, using the job description.

Ensure that employees have the knowledge, skills, and confidence to do their jobs through orientation and training.

Continually coach employees.

Formally evaluate their performance at least once yearly.

Use corrective action or discipline when necessary.

Each of these topics will be discussed in this chapter. But before we start, there is one more thing you need to ensure that your employees do their jobs well. You need to believe that most employees want to do a good job, that most employees really do care. People tend to conform to your expectations about them. If you treat your employees as lazy and irresponsible individuals, they will probably be just like that. However, if you give your employees the impression that they can do a great job, they probably will.

13. Use Up-to-Date and Accurate Job Descriptions

When formulated properly, job descriptions let employees know what is expected of them. They explain the what, how, why, and where of a job, as seen in Fig. 3-1. The *what* refers to the nature of the duties and tasks an employee performs. For example, a server greets and serves guests. *How* refers to the techniques and methods, materials and equipment, and guidelines involved in a job. For example, a server serves guests according to service standards. The *why* of the job refers to the purpose or results of the job duties. When a server serves guests, the desired result is the guest's return visit.

In addition to outlining job duties, each job description should include a section on professional conduct. This section addresses the ways in which employees are to interact with each other and with guests, how they are to be dressed, the importance of getting to work

Fig. 3-1 JOB DESCRIPTION

JOB DESCRIPTION

JOB IDENTIFICATION

Job Title: Cook

Department: Kitchen Reports to: Chef

Hours: 9:00 A.M.–5:00 P.M. or 2:00 P.M.–10:00 P.M.

Exempt or Nonexempt: Nonexempt

Grade: 8

JOB SUMMARY

Prepares all menu items to facility standards and in a timely manner

RESULTS AND DUTIES

1. Prepares tasty foods for guests under the guidance of the Chef
   a. Uses and follows recipes
   b. Adjusts recipes accurately
   c. Uses high-quality ingredients and measures them accurately
   d. Operates all kitchen equipment correctly
   e. Taste tests and evaluates foods before serving to make sure standards are met; consults with Chef if has any concerns
   f. Portions food into standard portions
   g. Garnishes food in appealing manner

2. Uses and maintains production records to prevent waste
   a. Uses and follows production sheets
   b. Keeps written records of all food produced
   c. Keeps written records of all foods left over

Fig. 3-1 Continued

3. Serves food that is safe to eat
   a. Follows facility's safe food-handling guidelines.
   b. Cleans and sanitizes work area according to cleaning schedule

4. Works as a team member to maintain pleasant work environment
   a. Comes to work on time
   b. Is not absent from work excessively
   c. Reports to work dressed according to the dress code
   d. Follows behavior standards
   e. Performs other duties as requested

JOB SETTING

Contacts: Other cooking staff, chef, servers, cleaning crew, storekeeper

Working Conditions: Works in hot area with much humidity at times; area becomes congested and noisy during busy times

Physical Demands: Is standing most of time; does much walking; frequently does heavy lifting

Work Hazards: Hot surfaces, steam, wet floors, hot grease, heavy lifting, knives and other sharp objects, electrical shocks

Fig. 3-1 Continued

JOB QUALIFICATIONS

Knowledge: Cooking terminology and ingredients

Skills and Abilities: Measures; uses a knife; identifies and uses various pieces of small and large kitchen equipment; reads and follows recipes; does basic math (addition, subtraction, multiplication, and division); uses any cooking method; determines degree of doneness in cooked foods; uses portion control tools; garnishes; works well with others; dresses per policy; is honest; handles stress; works hard; is reliable

Work Experience: One year of satisfactory experience as a cook required; two to three years cooking experience preparing a variety of menu items preferred

Education and Training: Culinary training preferred

Incumbent Signature: ______________________ Date: __________

Approval Signature: ______________________ Date: __________

Approval Signature: ______________________ Date: __________

and being on time, and anything else that contributes to a positive work environment.

A job description should include the following sections: job identification, job summary, results and duties, and job setting. In some cases, job qualifications may also be included. Job descriptions are discussed in detail, and many samples given, in *Staffing Your Foodservice Operation,* the first book in this series.

Job descriptions are valuable tools for laying out performance expectations for your employees and for evaluating performance. Job descriptions can also be used to help in career guidance of employees.

Guidelines for Using Job Descriptions to Manage Performance

- The job applicant should be made familiar with the job description at some point during the staffing process. Typically, a job description is discussed with each applicant during the interview. In this manner, performance expectations are laid out *before* hiring so that there are no surprises later for either the employee or the manager.
- The job description should be discussed with each new employee during orientation and a written copy given to each new hire.
- Because it describes what an employee does, use a job description as the foundation for job training and formal performance review programs.

Job descriptions should be reviewed once yearly for accuracy and modified when necessary.

14. Orient New Employees

Research provides increasing evidence that a lack of orientation or poor orientation contributes to new hires' dissatisfaction and turnover. For new hires, the first 30 days are likely to be the most crucial. Without orientation, employees take longer to become proficient in their new positions and make more mistakes. Yet every day a nervous foodservice employee starts a new job with little instruction or guidance. Foodservice managers are quite concerned about guests feeling comfortable while dining in their establishments; they need to be equally concerned about their new employees feeling comfortable. After all, the way employees treat guests is often a reflection of how they are treated by management.

An orientation program sends a message to new hires that you care about how they do their jobs and that their jobs are important. Orientation also communicates to employees what is expected of them and gives them the big picture of how their jobs fit into the overall mission of the company. Use your orientation program as a way to put your new employees at ease and to give them a good first impression of your company; remember, you may not get a second chance to make a favorable impression.

A new employee needs to be oriented in three different areas: the company, its pertinent policies and procedures, and the new job. Following are common orientation topics included in each of these three areas.

THE COMPANY

Description of the company, including history and operation (type of menu, service, hours of operation, etc.)
Vision statement and guiding principles
Organizational structure (including to whom the employee reports and to whom his or her boss reports)

POLICIES AND PROCEDURES

Dress code and uniforms
Parking
Signing or clocking in
Lockers
Time off, including sick time, holiday time, personal time, and vacation time as applicable
Call-in policy for illness, emergencies, etc.
Requesting time off
Salary, overtime, and tip reporting
Paychecks
Benefits
Personal use of telephone
Smoking
Meals
Communication channels
Disciplinary guidelines
Guest relations
Teamwork
Property removal
Responsible service of alcohol
Equal Employment Opportunity
Promotions and transfers
Professional conduct or behavior standards
Safe food handling and on-the-job safety

THE NEW JOB
Tour of the operation and introduction to co-workers and managers
Work schedule, including hours of work, days off, and break times
Job description and standards of performance
Training program
Probationary period
Employee evaluation

Once a list like this has been developed, managers can use it as a checklist in orienting each new employee. The benefit of using such a checklist is that it ensures consistency among managers who are conducting orientation and makes it unlikely that any topic will be forgotten.

In addition to the checklist, it is a good idea to develop and distribute to each new employee an employee handbook, sometimes called a personnel handbook. An employee handbook covers all policies and procedures with which employees need to become familiar. Because employees are likely to forget much of what is said about policies and procedures during orientation, the employee handbook is a valuable reference for them to use later. Employees should be asked to sign, either on a covering page in the employee handbook, which is turned in to Personnel, or on the orientation checklist, documenting that they have been given this information.

How long should orientation last? The only guideline here is that orientation is complete when the new employee has a sense of belonging, is committed to the goals of the work group and the overall mission, and is proficient on the job. The next section addresses job training for the new employee.

Following is a summary of the steps in orienting new employees to the foodservice operation.

1. With managerial and employee input, develop an orientation checklist.
2. Develop an employee handbook covering anything your new hires need to know about the operation.
3. Determine who will do the orientation, when it will be done, and how long it will last. Often each of the three segments of training (the company, the policies and procedures, the new job) are done by the new hire's immediate supervisor during the first few days of work. The length of time will vary tremendously depending on what will be covered. In some cases, company orientation is done separately from the other two segments. When a new employee starts work, he or she is normally quite anxious to fit into the new

job and work group, so it is probably better to conduct company orientation when the employee feels comfortable on the job.

4. Train your managers to use the orientation checklist to conduct orientations. Emphasize the importance of greeting each new employee warmly, developing rapport, and asking questions of the new employee to ascertain understanding during the orientation itself.
5. During the orientation process, ask new employees how they think their training is progressing. Solicit their comments and concerns. Ask them to identify areas in which they feel competent and not so competent. Do so at least weekly until they are fully functioning.

15. Train Employees to Do Their Jobs Well

Training means to instruct and guide the development of a trainee toward acquiring knowledge, behavior or skills, and attitudes to meet specific needs. The overall goal of training is to bring about a desired level of work performance. Orienting new employees to the company is one specific focus of training. Training may also focus on

Helping new employees perform their new jobs well
Helping existing employees perform their current jobs well
Promoting employee involvement
Helping employees qualify for future jobs
Keeping employees informed of changes
Providing opportunities for personal development

Without proper job training, employees often feel incompetent, become frustrated, and may leave. With job training, the possibility of retaining employees increases, as well as the possibility of deriving other benefits, as follows:

Good job performance
Consistently high quality of food and service
Increased job satisfaction and morale
Less absenteeism
Fewer accidents
Less waste and breakage
More time for management to manage
Improved communication
Improved employee self-image

Despite the benefits of training, it remains neglected in many foodservice operations. How many times have you seen a new employee report for duty and immediately be told to work with another employee who has little desire to train another person in addition to performing his or her own job? Although training requires a time commitment, it is preferable and less costly in the long run than recruiting, evaluating, and selecting new employees.

HOW EMPLOYEES LEARN BEST

Before considering how to develop training programs, it is important to examine seven ways by which employees learn best.

1. When employees participate in their own training, they tend to identify with and retain the concepts being taught. To get employees involved, choose appropriate training methods. See page 47 for a description of various training methods that promote employee involvement.
2. Employees learn best when training material is practical, relevant, useful, and geared to an appropriate level. Learning is facilitated, too, when the material is well organized and presented in small, easy-to-grasp steps. Adult learners are selective about what they will spend time learning, and learning must be especially pertinent and rewarding for them. Adults also need to be able to master new skills at their own pace.
3. Employees learn best in an informal, quiet, and comfortable setting. Your effort in selecting and maintaining an appropriate training environment shows employees that you think their training is important. When employees are stuffed into a crowded office or a noisy part of the kitchen, or when the trainer is interrupted by phone calls, they may rightly feel that their training isn't really important. Employees like to feel special; so, when possible, find a quiet setting. Of course, much training, such as on-the-job training, necessarily takes place in the work environment.
4. Employees learn best when they are being paid for time spent in training.
5. Employees learn best with a good trainer. Although you may not ever find a person with all these qualities, you can use this list to evaluate potential trainers.

Characteristics of a Successful Trainer

- Is knowledgeable
- Displays enthusiasm

- Has a sense of humor
- Communicates clearly, concisely, straightforwardly
- Is sincere, caring, respectful, responsive to employees
- Encourages employee performance; is patient
- Sets an appropriate role model
- Is well organized
- Maintains control, frequent eye contact with employees
- Listens well
- Is friendly and outgoing
- Keeps calm; is easygoing
- Tries to involve all employees
- Facilitates learning process
- Positively reinforces employees

6. Employees learn best when they receive awards or incentives. For example, on successful completion of training for the position of cook, you can send a letter of recognition to the employee, which can also be put into the personnel file. The largest franchisee of Arby's awards employees a progression of bronze, silver, and gold name tags, as well as pay increases, as they learn each area of the restaurant. When the employee has learned all areas, he or she is promoted to the position of crew leader.
7. Employees learn best when they are coached on their performance. Coaching is discussed in the next section.

THE TRAINING PROGRAM

Once you have decided that you will train your employees, you will need to develop and implement an orientation program, as discussed earlier. Next you will need to develop a job skills program to train new employees and retrain current employees. Both orientation and job skills programs should include the following components.

1. Measurable performance objectives—what new knowledge, behaviors, or attitudes the employees will acquire
2. Content—what is to be taught
3. Delivery—how it will be taught
4. Schedule—when and for how long training will take place
5. Trainers—who will be responsible for the training

JOB SKILLS TRAINING

Most job skills training is accomplished through one or more of the following formats.

- Group training
- Learner-controlled instruction
- Individual training or on-the-job training

Group training refers to training two or more employees typically in a classroom environment. It is useful in training two or more employees in the same task, or groups of employees in human relations skills, such as handling guest complaints. Group training is also useful in creating and maintaining a positive organizational climate, such as in company orientation. Appendix B contains two training outlines used by a trainer for group instruction.

Learner-controlled instruction is largely done without a trainer. For example, some foodservice chains have interactive computer programs or videotape presentations that the learner uses for training in a variety of areas. This type of instruction is quite useful in teaching standardized procedures because of its high degree of consistency. It is also convenient for the employee, who can pick a convenient time to use it, and for the manager, who is freed from some training responsibilities. On the other hand, learner-controlled instruction is costly to develop and to revise when procedures change.

On-the-job training (OJT) is the most widely used method of job skills training and retraining. With this method, the employee is placed into the real work situation and trained to do the various parts of a job by an experienced employee or supervisor. OJT provides application and satisfaction for an anxious new employee and, when done correctly, is very effective. OJT works best when the following conditions are met.

- The trainer must be willing and able to train a new employee. If the trainer is an hourly employee, you can provide incentive by compensating him or her through a pay increase for the hours spent training, a new title, or some other mark of distinction.
- Training should be structured and specific tasks to be learned designated. An OJT checklist (see Fig. 3-2) should be used by the trainer to direct activities. To develop an OJT checklist, list the tasks involved for each job duty given in the job description. The steps involved in each task, such as setting a table, need to be provided in written form for reference. Frequently these procedures are found in a training manual or operations manual. The OJT checklist may also specify the order in which tasks are to be learned, as well as the time required.
- Duties, along with their rationale and performance standards, should be taught. Performance standards are observable and

Fig. 3-2 ON-THE-JOB TRAINING CHECKLIST

OJT CHECKLIST—COOK

Name of Trainee: ______________________________

Date Starting Training: ______________________________

Trainer(s): ______________________________

Write the date in the blank space next to each task when you feel the trainee has mastered it.

Prepares Food

_______ Uses production sheet
_______ Locates and uses recipes
_______ Adjusts recipes
_______ Gathers necessary supplies
_______ Operates kitchen equipment
_______ Times food preparation
_______ Portions food
_______ Garnishes food
_______ Serves an acceptable product
_______ Keeps written records of all food produced and leftovers
_______ Follows safe food-handling guidelines
_______ Handles leftovers
_______ Cleans and sanitizes work area using cleaning schedule

General

_______ Dresses according to dress code
_______ Is hospitable and courteous toward guests
_______ Comes to work and is on time
_______ Works as a team member

Please sign below upon completion of training. Both the employee and the trainer certify by their signatures that the training has been adequate to prepare the new employee to function in his or her new position.

______________________________ ______________________________

Signature/Date (Employee) Signature/Date (Trainer)

measurable criteria from which to decide whether a job duty is being done correctly. For example, requiring a server to greet guests with a smile, and within 2 minutes of their being seated, is a performance standard. Standards help employees to know whether they are doing their jobs correctly.

- The trainer should be patient, clear, and supportive, and use the Tell/Show/Do/Review technique to teach the steps involved in various duties.

Following are 15 steps to follow when using the Tell/Show/Do/Review training method.

TELL

1. Tell the employee: "The job duty you are going to learn is. . . ." Use language appropriate to the skill level of the employee.
2. Find out what the employee already knows about the task.
3. Explain the steps involved in the job duty and its overall purpose.

SHOW

4. Demonstrate the procedure in order, explaining what, why, and how well to do each step.
5. Instruct at a rate that allows the employee to comprehend the task.
6. Instruct clearly and completely.
7. Encourage questions from the employee.

DO

8. Let the employee do the job.
9. Give frequent, specific, and accurate feedback.
10. Correct in a calm, positive, and friendly way.
11. Praise and give encouragement.
12. Ask questions to keep the employee's attention, get him or her thinking, assess understanding, and increase retention.

    "Why did you. . . ?"
    "What would happen if. . . ?"
    "What would you do if. . . ?"
    "How will you. . . ?"

    Also ask the employee for his or her feelings about how he or she is doing.

REVIEW

13. Review the what, how, and why of the job duty, continuing to ask questions of the employee.
14. Encourage further questions from the employee.
15. Put the employee on his or her own and coach. Be available for the employee to ask questions. Be supportive. (Coaching is the next topic to be discussed.)

TRAINING METHODS THAT PROMOTE EMPLOYEE INVOLVEMENT

In a *demonstration,* a trainer shows an employee how to perform a certain skill or procedure, such as to set up a three-compartment sink. This is a useful way to teach manual skills. Demonstrations can also be used to focus attention on basic procedures and to teach certain standards of performance.

Guidelines for Demonstration

- Run through the demonstration beforehand and make sure you are totally comfortable and competent at the task.
- Explain why each step is done as you do it.
- Point out critical parts of the procedure.
- Do not demonstrate too many steps at once.
- Teach in small, easy-to-grasp steps.
- Follow with supervised practice by employees.

The four components of this method—lecture (tell), demonstration (show), do (employee practice), and lecture (review)—provide an excellent strategy for teaching a new skill or procedure. Employees are able to practice and apply knowledge and skills, previous explained and demonstrated, under controlled conditions and close supervision.

Guidelines for Tell/Show/Do/Review

- Employees should have a listing of procedures either in hand or posted so they can follow them during practice.
- Small groups are best.
- Supervise closely and correct employees quickly.
- Be sure all safety aspects of the process have been thoroughly discussed and demonstrated.
- Give employees enough practice time to be proficient.
- Allow enough time for this method—it can be quite time-consuming.

A *game* is a structured competition designed to provide opportunities to bring out specific knowledge. It might be a board game or created in any situation in which employees work alone or (usually) in teams and compete with each other for a prize of some type. The contest is governed by a set of rules. Games, when well designed, are participative, well accepted by employees, and represent a change of pace. For example, you could ask employees to form groups of two to four people. Now read a series of questions to all groups, allowing 1 minute for each to write down an answer. Award one point for each correct answer, and keep a record of each group's score. At the end, add up each group's points, and award a prize to the group with the most points.

Guidelines for a Game

- Make sure that rules are explicit and communicated well.
- Offer a prize that is desired by most of the employees playing the game and that is of appropriate value.
- When employees pick their own teams, make sure everyone is on a team.
- Make sure there is enough time to complete the game once it is started.

Employees split into small *buzz groups* of two to four people to discuss a specific topic, and are then asked to report the key discussion points back to the larger group. The trainer may write down these points on a chalkboard or easel pad.

Guidelines for Buzz Groups

- As for all group discussions, monitor the groups to make sure they have not wandered off track.
- If any group members are not participating at all, ask questions that will involve them in the discussion.
- Make sure each group has a person recording the discussion.
- When writing key discussion points on the chalkboard, either write each group's points separately or put all groups' points together. Do not write the same response twice. If a group gives a response that differs only in wording, explain that the point has already been noted.
- Give adequate time for all groups to respond.

A *case study* is a description of a real-life situation, event, or incident that an employee or group of employees analyzes and discusses, usually through answering specific questions. Such a study allows for analysis of information and opportunity to use newly acquired skills and knowledge. The answers to the questions should be discussed in class. Follow the guidelines for buzz groups.

In a *role play* employees simulate or act out a real or hypothetical situation involving two or more people such as handling a customer complaint. This technique can be used to examine current behaviors or try new ones to build skill and confidence. It is usually followed by analysis and discussion among participants. Role plays enable evaluation and coaching by peers and the trainer.

Guidelines for Role Play

- Always demonstrate a role play first before employees try one themselves.
- Understand that some employees will think role-playing is silly; explain to them that it gives them a chance to try out a new behavior in a relatively safe situation.
- Keep group size small.
- Coach closely.
- Give lots of positive reinforcement and correct tactfully.

In a *simulation,* the actual work environment is duplicated as much as possible. Employees are guided to safely try out new behaviors. For example, an employee may be asked to ring up sales on a computerized cash register set up on a table. Follow the guidelines for role play.

16. Coach Your Employees

Coaching is a two-part process: observation of employee performance, and conversation about job performance between manager and employee. The overall goals of the conversation are to evaluate work performance, then to encourage optimum work performance by either reinforcing good performance or confronting and redirecting poor performance. Coaching therefore provides employees with regular support and feedback about job performance and alerts the manager to exactly what employees need to know.

If coaching employees is so beneficial, why do managers often avoid it? Here are some possible reasons.

- Lack of time
- Fear of confronting an employee with a concern about performance
- Assumption that the employee already knows he or she is doing a good job
- Little experience in doing or observing coaching
- Assumption that the employee will ask questions when appropriate and does not need feedback

The first step in coaching is to observe employees doing their jobs. If an employee is doing a job well, do not hesitate to tell the employee. Everyone likes to be told that he or she is doing a good job, so praise employees as often as you can, preferably while observing them and in front of their peers. Work on catching your employees doing things right, then use these steps.

1. Describe the specific praiseworthy action.
2. Explain the results or effects of the action.
3. State your appreciation.
4. Ask the employee how he or she feels about doing a good job.
5. Say thank you.
6. Write a letter of thanks and make sure a copy goes into the employee's personnel file (see Fig. 3-3).

If there appears to be a problem with some aspect of the employee's performance, consider the following questions.

What is the difference between the employee's performance level and the performance standard? Is it significant?
Is the performance standard realistic?
Does the employee know *what* is supposed to be done?
Does the employee understand *why* it is supposed to be done?
Does the employee know *how* it is supposed to be done?
Are there any hindrances to the employee's performance that the employee cannot control, such as inadequate equipment?
Has the employee received feedback on this problem earlier, or has the problem been ignored?

The next step is to confront, not criticize, the employee's poor performance. Confronting is a positive process used to correct performance problems, gain the employee's commitment to improvement, and maintain a constructive supervisor-employee relationship. Criticism, on the other hand, is a negative process which, instead of con-

Fig. 3-3 LETTER OF THANKS TO EMPLOYEE

Thank-You Memorandum

TO: Tony Smith, Dishwasher
FROM: Tom Jones, Manager
DATE: 7/12/91

Thank you for doing such a great job last night when the dishwasher broke down during the dinner rush. You very calmly informed your supervisor so a phone call could be made immediately to the repair company. Then you set up the three-compartment sink correctly and continued washing dishes until the job was done. Thanks for using your head and making sure the job was done right. We all appreciate what you did!

cc: Personnel file

centrating on performance, involves blaming the employee personally for not doing a job properly. It tends to be general rather than specific in nature, and generates excuses, blaming of others, and guilt on the employee's part. Managers who confront employees are interested in helping them feel confident about improving future performance, rather than making them feel inadequate and guilty about past performance.

When confronting an employee with what is perceived to be a performance problem, follow these steps.

1. Speak in private with the employee and identify the area of concern by saying, for instance, "I am concerned about . . ." or "I need your help with. . . ." Describe the employee's behavior objectively and in concrete terms. Do not use vague terms, guess the employee's motives, or generalize that "You *always* do this."
2. Encourage the employee to discuss how he or she sees the situation by using the seven questions just listed (page 50) as a starting point. Following are sample questions.

   "Do you know how to clean up that area properly?"
   "Is there anything keeping you from doing the job properly?"
   "Did you know that was part of your job?"
   "Do you know why that part of your job is so important?"
3. Summarize the employee's remarks to ensure that you correctly understand what he or she has told you.
4. Mutually discuss ways of eliminating the problem by stating, for example, "In the future, how can we prevent this from happening?" At this stage the problem is often quickly resolved because the employee simply was not aware of something and readily agrees to correct the situation. At other times the employee may not readily own up to the performance problem and you will need to actively seek his or her ideas and suggestions and possibly make suggestions of your own.
5. Mutually agree on an action plan, making sure that all actions to be taken are realistic, specific, measurable, documented, and have clearly defined follow-up dates.
6. To check his or her understanding, ask the employee to restate what has been agreed upon. Show enthusiasm for the plan and be supportive.
7. Close the discussion by stating your confidence in the employee's ability to improve the situation.

Be sure to follow up with the employee on the appropriate date to evaluate performance.

General Coaching Guidelines

- Be specific and accurate about job performance.
- Actively listen to the employee. Be supportive and objective. Do not let the conversation drift away to other issues or discussion of other employees. If the conversation starts to drift, make a statement such as "Let's get back to the issue at hand."
- Focus on the employee's behavior, not on the employee. Always affirm the self-respect and self-esteem of the employee.
- The most effective time to reinforce positive performance is while the desired behavior is occurring. If that is not possible, the next best time is immediately afterwards. Confront job performance as soon as possible after observing it. However, if you are at all angry or upset, do not confront the employee. Wait until you are calm.
- Correct in private. Employees are very sensitive about being corrected in front of their peers. Unless the error could have grave consequences, wait until you can at least take the employee aside long enough to tell him or her how to correct it.
- Explain the impact of the employee's job performance on the work group and the total operation.
- Be a coach, not a drill sergeant. Do not stay constantly at a person's side, watching everything he or she does.

17. Formally Evaluate Employee Performance at Least Once Yearly

Performance appraisal, the periodic evaluation of an employee's job performance, is one of the most negatively viewed and poorly performed managerial tasks. Ron Zemke of *Training* magazine states, "Performance appraisals are about as beloved as IRS audits . . . evidence has been popping up to suggest that most performance appraisal systems are more noteworthy for the angst they create than the results they achieve." Managers and subordinates alike generally dislike performance appraisal programs and interviews. Managers often view the performance appraisal program as time-consuming (which it often is), are doubtful that positive results will follow, and hesitate to tell employees that there are aspects of job performance that need improvement. Likewise, employees feel that they do not get a chance to say much (which is usually true), that the boss is not prepared, that they are being evaluated unfairly, and that the appraisal emphasizes the negative rather than the positive.

Evaluation of job performance is much more than an annual perfor-

Fig. 3-4 PERFORMANCE MANAGEMENT CYCLE

mance appraisal. It is a managerial function and responsibility and is the key to retaining, utilizing, and developing employees. Companies that realize this have replaced performance appraisal programs with performance management programs (see Fig. 3-4). In addition to reviewing performance at specific intervals (traditionally once a year), they have instituted ongoing coaching of employees. Thus the yearly performance appraisal is less likely to create anxiety, because performance is monitored more closely.

Performance appraisals have various roles or uses in foodservice operations. A performance appraisal gives the employee an answer to the question "How well am I doing?" It not only provides an opportunity to offer the employee feedback on how well he or she is meeting standards, but also to communicate on other performance issues. If problem areas of work performance are identified, the employee may be advised to undergo training. Very often the performance appraisal is the basis for an employee's salary increase (referred to as pay for performance) and possible promotion. Opportunities for career and personal development can be discussed at the time of the appraisal. When conducted appropriately, performance appraisals can also enhance employees' satisfaction and motivation.

For the organization, performance appraisals are used to improve communication and manager/employee relationships, remind employees of the company's goals and missions, determine training needs, and improve performance. Such results may then lead to increased morale and decreased turnover.

PERFORMANCE STANDARDS AND APPRAISAL FORMS

The first step in any performance appraisal system is the development of performance standards against which performance will be measured. Performance standards (or criteria) translate job duties into levels of acceptable or unacceptable performance. For example, a performance standard for servers might read: "Greets customers within three minutes of their being seated." Performance standards should be job-based, observable, measurable, and realistic.

Performance standards may involve quantity, such as the number of covers or tables a server can take care of, or quality, such as the percent of orders taken without error. Standards may also address speed or cost. The use of vague words such as *approximately, appropriate, reasonable,* and *adequate* should be avoided. Figure 3-5 is a performance appraisal form that includes performance standards.

Another popular way to evaluate employees uses the graphic rating scale. Figure 3-6 depicts a scale that, although still often used, has some serious handicaps. In its left-hand column are categories of job duties and responsibilities, also called performance dimensions, such as job knowledge and quality of work. To the right are rating or response categories, such as outstanding or unsatisfactory.

Performance dimensions are often based on personality traits considered important to good job performance, such as dependability, ability to communicate well, and cooperation. The use of such traits in job evaluations should be avoided unless they can be defined in terms of observable, job-related behavior. For instance, dependability can be rephrased as "comes to work on time."

Another problem with this sample graphic rating scale is that the rating categories are ambiguous and could be interpreted quite differently by two different raters. Rating categories should be behaviorally based, unambiguous, and relevant to the dimensions being rated. In general, five to nine response categories produce the most consistent ratings. For example, response categories for the performance dimension "ability to adjust and use recipes" may range from "employee accurately adjusts recipes and follow instructions precisely" to "employee frequently makes errors adjusting and following recipes."

To be used successfully, performance appraisal forms need to be

- Easy to understand and use
- Acceptable to the evaluators
- Acceptable to the employees (they should be involved in their development)
- Communicated to employees during orientation
- Revised periodically

RATING ERRORS

The rater or evaluator has the responsibility of rating an employee's performance and communicating the evaluation to the employee.

Fig. 3-5 PERFORMANCE APPRAISAL FORM

SERVER PERFORMANCE EVALUATION

Name: ____________________

Position: ____________________

Date of Hire: __________ Yearly or 60-Day Evaluation: __________

Department: ____________________

Please use COMMENT section whenever "Exceeds" or "Does Not Meet" is checked. POINTS: Exceeds—5, Meets—3, Does not meet—0.

Performance Standards	Exceeds	Meets	Does Not Meet
1. Stocks the service station for one serving area for one meal completely and correctly, as specified on the Service Station Procedures Sheet, in 10 minutes or less.	______	______	______
	Comments:		
2. Sets or resets a table properly, as shown on the Table Setting Layout Sheet, in not more than 3 minutes.	______	______	______
	Comments:		
3. Greets guests cordially within 5 minutes after they are seated and takes their order if time permits; if too busy, informs then that he or she will be back as soon as possible.	______	______	______
	Comments:		
4. Explains menu to customers: accurately describes the day's specials and, if asked, accurately answers any questions on portion size, ingredients, taste, and preparation method.	______	______	______
	Comments:		

Performance Standards	Exceeds	Meets	Does Not Meet
5. Takes food, wine, and beverage orders accurately and legibly for a table of up to six guests according to Guest Check Procedures; prices and totals check with 100 percent accuracy.	______ Comments:	______	______
6. Picks up order and completes plate preparation according to Plate Preparation Procedure.	______ Comments:	______	______
7. Serves a complete meal to all persons at each table in an assigned station in not more than 1 hour per table using the Tray Service Procedures.	______ Comments:	______	______
8. If asked, recommends wines appropriate to menu items selected, according to the What Wine Goes with What Food Sheet; opens and serves wines correctly as shown on the Wine Service Sheet.	______ Comments:	______	______
9. Accepts and processes payment with 100 percent accuracy as specified on the Check Payment Procedures Sheet.	______ Comments:	______	______
10. Performs side work correctly according to the Side Work Assignments Sheet and as requested.	______ Comments:	______	______
11. Operates all equipment in assigned area according to the Safety Manual.	______ Comments:	______	______

Fig. 3-5 Continued

Performance Standards	Exceeds	Meets	Does Not Meet
12. Meets at all times the Dress Code requirements.	______ Comments:	______	______
13. Uses at all times the sanitation procedures specified for serving personnel in the Sanitation Manual; maintains work area to score 90 percent or higher on the Sanitation Checklist.	______ Comments:	______	______
14. Maintains a "Good" or higher rating on the Customer Relations Checklist; maintains a customer complaint ratio of less than 1 per 200 customers served.	______ Comments:	______	______
15. Maintains a check average of not less than $7 per person at lunch and $15 per person at dinner.	______ Comments:	______	______
16. Is absent from work less than 12 days in a year.	______ Comments:	______	______
17. Is late to work less than 12 times in a year.	______ Comments:	______	______
18. Can always be found in work area during work hours or supervisor knows where he or she is.	______ Comments:	______	______
19. Attends or makes up all required meetings and training.	______ Comments:	______	______
20. Supervisor receives positive feedback from peers with minimal complaints	______ Comments:	______	______

Fig. 3-5 Continued

OVERALL RATING:

Outstanding Performance: 75–100 points (must meet or exceed all standards)

Good Performance: 50–74 points

Marginal Performance, Reevaluate in 60 Days: Below 50 points

EVALUATOR'S COMMENTS: ____________________

____

____

EMPLOYEE'S COMMENTS: Please comment freely on this evaluation.

____

____

____

EMPLOYEE'S OBJECTIVES: What would you like to accomplish in the next 12 months? ____________________

____

____

EMPLOYEE'S OBJECTIVES FOR THE NEXT 12 MONTHS:

(Plan should be specific, realistic, measurable, and include target dates.)

____

____

____

SIGNATURES:

____________________	____________________	____________________
Employee	Evaluator	Reviewer

Date:____________________

Fig. 3-6 GRAPHIC RATING SCALE

Factors	Unsatisfactory	Conditional	Average	Above Average	Outstanding
Quality of work					
Quantity of work					
Job knowledge					
Cooperation					
Dependability					
Attendance					
Appearance					
Get along with others					

Raters should receive training in both these areas as they require certain skills. Six common rating errors are described here.

1. A major error in rating employee performance is making *subjective evaluations.* Being objective is difficult because each evaluator brings to the rating process his or her own attitudes, values, perceptions, prejudices, stereotypes, and emotions. Objective evaluation starts with appraising an employee's performance, not the employee.
2. The *halo effect* refers to allowing the rating of one area in which an employee does very well, such as being cooperative, to positively influence the rating of other areas. For example, a cook who does very well in the area of practicing good sanitation and always has a neat, clean appearance, may also be rated highly on his ability to produce high-quality food, when, in fact, this is not the case. The opposite of the halo effect is the *horns effect,* by which a poor rating in one aspect of the evaluation negatively influences the rating of other factors.
3. The *error of central tendency* occurs when evaluators tend to rate everyone about the same because of an inclination to avoid extremes when rating anything. Typically, employees are ranked as average or just above average.
4. *Leniency error* occurs when the evaluator is too generous with ratings because of a tendency to want to be everyone's friend, to avoid the unpleasant tasks of confronting and discussing performance problems and dealing with employee defensiveness. Evaluators inflate ratings for other reasons as well: to avoid confronting poor performance with hard-to-manage employees, to help someone whose work performance is declining as a result of personal problems, to make the department look good, to make

sure an employee gets a decent raise, or to encourage an employee whose overall performance is poor, but who has made much recent progress. Such leniency may result in a problem for the company. Should a well-rated employee's performance slip, and he or she is fired, the employee, if the the case is taken to court, could win the decision when his or her many "good" evaluations are brought to light. Another problem with leniency arises when employees are not told of their deficiencies. As a result, their performance and productivity do not improve, and they are less likely to be promoted. The opposite of leniency error is *severity error,* in which everyone is rated poorly. The reason for such error may be that the rater is a perfectionist and few employees measure up to his or her stringent interpretation of performance standards.

5. *Recency error* occurs when the employee is rated only on his or her most recent performance. Performance review does not begin a month before the yearly review session; it actually starts a full year earlier. Recency error occurs frequently because the rater has insufficient and/or erroneous documentation of employee performance so that only vague, general statements, based on recent observations, are written. Such negligence upsets the employee especially when incidents of outstanding performance are forgotten. Some employees are aware that their boss reviews only recent performance, so they save their energy and work diligently during just the last part of the appraisal period.
6. *First impression and fixed impression errors* both refer to a rater who has limited insight into an employee's performance. In first impression error, the evaluator rates an employee solely on his or her first impression of the employee, rather than on ongoing performance. In fixed impression error, the evaluator typically bases the performance evaluation on only a few observations of the employee.

In addition to these rating errors, length of service can affect ratings significantly. It is often difficult for raters to give a less-than-satisfactory rating to employees who have achieved many years of satisfactory service and/or previous good evaluations.

Guidelines for Evaluating an Employee's Performance

- Evaluate the performance, not the employee. Be objective.
- Give specific examples of performance to back up ratings.

- Where there is substandard performance, ask why. Use the "rule of finger," which means looking closely at yourself before blaming the employee. Perhaps the employee was not given enough training or the appropriate tools to do the job.
- Think of fairness and consistency when evaluating performance. Ask yourself, "If this were my review, how would I react?"
- Seek input from others who have a working relationship with the employee.

THE PERFORMANCE APPRAISAL INTERVIEW

The performance appraisal interview is an occasion to give encouragement and to work on improving performance and building commitment to the organization. If it has been a year since the last appraisal, it may be too late to give praise or to remedy past problems. This is a time to help, not reward or punish. Unfortunately, salary review is the major purpose and function of many performance appraisals. Whether happy or unhappy with the ratings, the employee tends to focus on the increase more than the evaluation. It is best to do two performance appraisals per year, 6 months apart—one for performance review and one for salary administration. A performance appraisal should also be done at the end of the probationary period of each new employee.

The performance appraisal interview includes preparation and the interview itself, as follows.

PREPARATION

1. Explain thoroughly to the employee, in advance, the performance appraisal instrument and interview process.
2. If applicable, ask the employee to rate him- or herself, using your standard evaluation form. Explain that the employee's feedback is important in this process and ask him or her to fill out the form as completely and honestly as possible.
3. Set an appropriate time for the interview that is convenient for the employee. Choose a place that is quiet and informal and where there will be no interruptions. Some employees find the boss's office to be intimidating, so you may want to arrange a neutral setting. Tell the employee where and when.
4. Review the entire file and fill out the performance appraisal form, using the employee's self-evaluation if you have it.
5. You may want to give the employee a copy of your completed performance appraisal a day or so before the interview. This allows the employee time to read and think about the evaluation, as well as to develop responses.

INTERVIEW

1. Establish and maintain a friendly, relaxed, trusting atmosphere by

   Sitting side by side
   Maintaining eye contact
   Explaining that honesty and feedback are important and that the discussion will be on performance, not personality
   Starting with a statement of purpose and agenda
   Reading employee nonverbal language for tension, anxiety, and misunderstanding
   Using positive, constructive language instead of negative language (Use words such as *concern* instead of *problem,* and *growth* instead of *shortcoming.*)
   Actively listening
   Being a coach instead of a judge
   Being constructive with your criticism
   Using specific examples and avoiding generalities
   Not allowing the conversation to drift to unrelated areas

2. Using the performance appraisal form (do not read directly from it), start with a discussion of employee strengths and give praise.
3. Next identify and ask for feedback on areas that need improvement. Be sure to cite specific examples of poor performance.
4. If the employee disagrees with your assessment of problem areas, listen and be open-minded enough to allow him or her to change your mind. The employee may let you know of situations of which you were not aware previously.
5. Strive to reach consensus on the areas that need improvement and a plan of action, or growth plan, to build the employee's strengths and overcome weaknesses. Make sure this plan includes deadlines and is specific, realistic, behavioral, measurable, consistent with the organization, and understood by the employee.
6. You may want to use this occasion to ask the employee for feedback on your own performance and/or comments on working conditions and supervisory relations.
7. Summarize and conclude on a positive note; for example, tell the employee how important his contribution is to the organization.

Some performance appraisal systems ask employees to fill out the appraisal form and evaluate themselves. Self-appraisal is surprisingly accurate. Many employees tend to underrate themselves, particularly the better employees; whereas less-effective employees may overrate themselves. If an employee is given a chance to participate, and the manager takes the self-appraisal seriously, the employee realizes that his opinion matters. The results may be less employee defensiveness, a more constructive performance appraisal interview, and improved motivation and job performance. Self-appraisal is particularly justified for an employee who works mainly without supervision.

18. Set Corrective Action Guidelines and Communicate Them to Employees

When your efforts at helping an employee improve performance are going nowhere, it is time to consider your last alternative, corrective action, more commonly known as discipinary action. The purpose of corrective action is to get the employee to take responsibility for his or her behavior and work on improving performance.

Corrective action guidelines describe the consequences of counterproductive behaviors, such as excessive tardiness or theft. Some operators first categorize these behaviors into minor infractions, major infractions, and causes for immediate discharge (Table 3-1). Minor infractions do little harm to the operation but can be serious if they are frequent or occur with other infractions. Examples include unexcused absences or latenesses, leaving the work area without permission, and taking long breaks. Major infractions interfere substantially with operations; they might include discourtesy to customers or refusal to perform a job duty. Causes for immediate discharge may be actions that are illegal, such as theft.

Strategy for Developing Corrective Action Guidelines

- It will be almost impossible to develop corrective action guidelines to cover all specific circumstances that may arise; make sure, however, that they are not too general.
- Write guidelines in clear, understandable language for both managers and employees. Have written copies available for all personnel.
- Punishment should fit the infraction and be reasonably related to the safe and efficient operation of the foodservice.
- Incorporate into your corrective action guidelines a progressive system that applies corrective measures in increasing degrees or steps. In a progressive system, an employee is rarely terminated for a first offense; instead the employee is given several opportunities to correct the behavior before suspension or termination is considered. The objective is to get the employee to correct behav-

Table 3-1 Corrective Action Guidelines

Type of Problem and Corrective Action	*Examples*
Minor infractions: will result in oral counseling and, if repeated, will lead to written warnings, suspension, and finally termination	Excessive absenteeism Excessive lateness Poor job performance Failure to report a work-related injury or accident promptly Improper use of company telephones Abuse of break times and meal periods Leaving assigned work area without supervisor's permission Violation or neglect of safety rules or contributing to hazardous conditions
Major infractions: will result in a written warning and possibly immediate suspension or termination	Refusal to carry out reasonable assignments from an authorized supervisor Discourteous treatment of guests or other employees, including harassing, coercing, threatening, or intimidating others Physical altercations Intoxication or incapacity on duty due to the use of alcohol or drugs Negligence that results in injury to oneself, another employee, or a guest Sleeping while on duty Fighting on company property
Causes for immediate discharge	Knowingly falsifying employment records such as time-worked records Unauthorized destruction or removal of company property Unauthorized punching of another employee's time card Possession, display, or use of firearms or other dangerous weapons while on company property Possession of alcohol or drugs while on company property

ior voluntarily. A progressive corrective action system often uses the following steps: verbal warning(s), written warning(s), suspension, and termination.

- Always include in your guidelines a procedure that allows for an employee to appeal a corrective action decision to someone other than the immediate boss, such as the next higher person in the chain of command or someone in the human resources or personnel department.
- Also include a time limit, and perhaps other conditions, under which corrective action documentation is removed from an employee's file. For example, you may specify that any documentation over 2 years old will be removed from the file. Employees often see such documentation as a hindrance to advancement or a satisfactory evaluation and may feel they have little reason to excel.

Adequate communication requires that corrective action guidelines be reviewed with new hires during orientation and with all employees at least annually, as a general reminder and as an opportunity for employees to ask questions. Be sure to explain the reasons for the guidelines. Employees are much more likely to follow rules when they know why they are important. A copy of your corrective action guidelines should also be posted on an employee bulletin board.

19. Handle Counterproductive Behaviors Using a Two-Step Process

When an unfortunate incident occurs, (for instance, if a customer complains about terrible service), do not rush to write up a corrective action warning until you have a good idea of what has happened. You may find yourself embarrassed should you pronounce an employee guilty, with documentation in hand, only to find that the employee was off on the day in question.

First, make an investigation in a timely manner. Get the facts; do not draw conclusions until all the facts are in. Remember, an employee is innocent until proven guilty.

When you have determined the identity of the employee involved in the incident, review his or her employment record, including recent performance evaluations and documentation of any previous problems. Discuss this person's performance and work record with other managers and human resource managers. Be sure to consider an employee's overall record and contributions.

As part of your investigation, you need to confront the employee with the incident to validate the facts. Of key importance is to approach the situation with an open mind and discuss it calmly and in a nonthreatening manner with the employee. State your concern and allow the employee to explain the situation from his or her point of view. Listen actively and get all the details. The employee may have a good explanation for what happened and may not be at fault.

The direction of the second step will depend on the results of your discussion with the employee. If the employee admits to committing an infraction, you will need to decide on the appropriate corrective action based on the employee's past record, the corrective action guidelines, and past practice. When informing the employee of the corrective action, it is important to ask him or her to suggest some solutions to the problem and a corrective plan of action. You can assist, but the primary responsibility in this phase lies with the employee, who needs to show a commitment to resolving the problem. Before ending the meeting, it is a good idea to ask the employee to restate his or her understanding of the problem and the plan of action. This helps to reinforce the employee's ownership of the problem. At this time, you need to set a follow-up date and inform the employee of what the next step will be if the problem is not corrected.

If, after discussing it with the employee, the situation remains unclear, you will need to do further research before reaching a decision on a course of action. Here are some important factors to review when considering corrective action.

- Evidence—Is there enough evidence to justify action?
- Extentuating circumstances—Was the problem caused largely by a situation beyond the employee's control?
- Employee's understanding of the rules—Did the employee understand the rules or procedures and the consequences for failing to follow them?
- Employee's past performance—Is this the first problem you have had with this employee, or one of many?
- Frequency and pattern—Has this problem occurred previously?
- Seriousness of the problem—What type of infraction is this? How seriously does it impact on the operation?
- Past practice—How have similar problems been handled? Have corrective actions been consistently enforced?

If you subsequently decide that there is a strong enough case to warrant corrective action, inform the employee and give the reasons for your decision. Again, ask the employee to develop a course of action to correct the problem, set up a date for follow-up, and tell the employee what the next step will be if the problem is not corrected.

Guidelines for Using Corrective Action

- Probably the most important issue to employees is whether management is fair and consistent in using corrective actions. Be sure to consult with appropriate personnel to ensure a fair and consistent system.
- Always express concern to your employee. Be positive and supportive. State your confidence in the employee's ability to improve.
- Always maintain the self-respect and self-esteem of the employee. Remember that your concern is with the individual's actions, not the individual.
- Use corrective actions in a timely manner. If you are annoyed or angry, wait until you are calm and in control.
- Always explain the appeals procedure and genuinely invite the employee to use it.
- Balance corrective action with positive reinforcement. When employees do things right, write them a thank-you or recognition memo.
- Always document corrective actions.

Documentation of corrective action is vital to generating employee understanding and motivation to work toward improvement. Figure 3-7 shows an example of documentation.

Tips on How to Document

- Document performance as quickly as possible. Make sure to include the date.
- Be specific about the employee's behavior and the circumstances under which it occurred. Be accurate and behavior-oriented. Document thoroughly and include answers to who, what, when, where, and how.
- Opinions and hearsay have no place in documentation. Note only facts, behavior, and direct observation. Be objective and clear.
- Be consistent by recording both positive and negative performance, and by documenting in the same manner for all employees.
- Document all information revealed in the investigation as well as that obtained from the employee during the interview.

Fig. 3-7 SAMPLE CORRECTIVE ACTION DOCUMENTATION

NOTICE OF CORRECTIVE ACTION

To: Larry Short, Cook
From: John White, Executive Chef
Date: 7/20/91

INFRACTION: Absent from work area during work time without permission

DATE OF INFRACTION: July 18, 1991

DESCRIPTION: On July 18th, at 10:00 you were supposed to be prepping foods for lunch service in the cooking area. I looked for you both inside and outside of the restaurant and asked around about where you were, but to no avail. At approximately 10:25 I saw you rushing into the Employee Entrance from your car. You told me you had an ''emergency'' and gave no details. You told me, as you did when a similar incident happened on June 10th, that you didn't have time to tell me you had to leave. As a result of your actions, your work gets behind and our lunch service gets off to a bad start. In the future, if you need to leave your station at a time other than break time, I expect to be asked. If this incident occurs again, the next step is a second written warning.

CORRECTIVE ACTION TAKEN:

- ___ Verbal Warning
- _X_ First Written Warning
- ___ Second Written Warning
- ___ Third Written Warning with Three Day Suspension
- ___ Termination

_______________ Supervisor's Signature

_______________ General Manager's Signature

Fig. 3-7 Continued

The contents of this have been reviewed with me.

____

Employee's Signature

TO THE EMPLOYEE: Please feel free to make comments in this space and/ or use the Appeals Procedure outlined in your Employee Handbook.

- Describe the significance of the behavior as compared with expected performance.
- Document any corrective action taken, the employee's plan for improvement, and the follow-up date.
- Always note the next step to be taken in the process if the employee does not improve.
- Employees should be asked to sign written documentation to confirm that it has been read to them. Be sure to inform employees clearly that signing the documentation signifies only their understanding of, not their agreement with, what is stated.
- Encourage employees to make written comments on all written corrective action notices.

20. Prevent Counterproductive Behaviors

The first step in preventing counterproductive behaviors is to do a good job in selecting employees. This topic is thoroughly discussed in the first book of this series, *Staffing Your Foodservice Operation.*

The second step in preventing disciplinary problems is to perform the various steps discussed in this chapter. Each step discussed here, starting with writing accurate and specific job descriptions, will help you communicate to employees what is expected of them.

The third step is to carefully select supervisors with good human relations skills. Training of supervisors to further develop these skills is also important.

Last, you need to listen actively to your employees and try to understand their needs. Each employee has his or her own expectations of a job, and it is your job to help your employees to meet their individual needs.

ASSESSMENT OF PERFORMANCE MANAGEMENT SKILLS

Directions: In the blank space at the front of each item, put the number which best indicates your estimation of the frequency of each behavior.

Scale: 5—Never, 4—Seldom, 3—Occasionally, 2—Usually, 1—Always

_____ 13. Use up-to-date and accurate job descriptions.
_____ 14. Orient new employees.
_____ 15. Train employees to do their jobs well.
_____ 16. Coach your employees.
_____ 17. Formally evaluate employee performance at least once yearly.
_____ 18. Set corrective action guidelines and communicate them to employees.
_____ 19. Handle counterproductive behaviors using a two-step process.
_____ 20. Prevent counterproductive behaviors.

The more frequently you use the above behaviors, the better you let employees know what is expected. In any case where you gave yourself a "3" or higher, use the following checklist to work harder on these skills.

PERFORMANCE MANAGEMENT SKILLS CHECKLIST

Directions: Use this checklist at periodic intervals, such as every month, to see how well you are doing in the selected skill areas. Check off the skills you used, as a way to reinforce your positive behaviors, and circle those skills you have not used but wish to. Keep this checklist handy as a reminder of the skills you want to work on.

13. Use up-to-date and accurate job descriptions.

    DID YOU:

    _____ Discuss the appropriate job description with each job applicant?
    _____ Discuss in depth the job description with each new hire and give him or her a copy?
    _____ Revise any job descriptions that were out-of-date and/or over one year old?

14. Orient new employees.

    DID YOU:

    _____ Greet each new employee warmly?
    _____ Use an orientation checklist that covered pertinent aspects of the company, policies and procedures, and the new job with all new employees?
    _____ Ask questions of the new employee to ascertain understanding?
    _____ Ask the new employee his or her thoughts on how orientation was going?
    _____ Hand out an employee or personnel handbook to all new employees?

15. Train employees to do their jobs well.

    DID YOU:

    _____ Provide an informal, quiet, and comfortable training setting as much as possible?
    _____ Ensure that the training material was practical, relevant, useful, and geared to an appropriate level?

PERFORMANCE MANAGEMENT SKILLS CHECKLIST Continued

_____ Ensure that the training material was well organized and presented in small, easy-to-grasp steps?
_____ Provide a trainer who wants to train, knows the material, is respected, and gets along well with others?
_____ Let employees participate in their training as much as possible?
_____ Provide rewards or incentives for the employees?
_____ Have OJT Checklists for the trainer and trainee to use?
_____ Communicate clearly the performance standards for the job?

16. Coach your employees.

DID YOU:

_____ Observe employees doing their jobs on a daily basis?
_____ Praise employees doing a good job?
_____ Praise in public?
_____ Confront employees who were having performance problems?
_____ Confront job performance as soon as possible after observing it?
_____ Confront in private?
_____ Consider that the employee may not know what to do, how to do it, or why it is supposed to be done (in the case of substandard performance)?
_____ Actively listen to the employee?
_____ Mutually discuss ways of eliminating performance concerns and agree on an action plan (when confronting an employee)?
_____ Speak to the employee using specific and accurate statements about job performance?
_____ Affirm the self-respect and self-esteem of the employee?

17. Formally evaluate employee performance at least once yearly.

DID YOU:

_____ Use appraisal forms that were communicated to the employees in advance?
_____ Use appraisal forms that were acceptable to the employees?
_____ Use appraisal forms that are easy to understand?
_____ Use performance standards that are job-based, observable, measurable, and realistic?

PERFORMANCE MANAGEMENT SKILLS CHECKLIST Continued

_____ Evaluate the performance, not the employee?
_____ Give specific examples of performance to back up ratings?
_____ Think about being fair and consistent when evaluating performance?
_____ Seek input from others who have a working relationship with the employee?
_____ Prepare for the performance appraisal interview by setting an appropriate time, choosing a quiet place, reviewing the employee's file and appraisal form, and obtaining the employee's self-appraisal (if applicable)?
_____ Establish a friendly, relaxed atmosphere for the appraisal?
_____ Actively listen?
_____ Act like a coach instead of a judge?
_____ Give constructive criticism?
_____ Give specific examples and avoid generalities?
_____ Focus the conversation?
_____ Mutually agree on areas of improvement?
_____ Mutually develop a plan of action that is specific, realistic, measurable, and includes deadlines?
_____ Summarize and conclude on a positive note?

18. Set corrective action guidelines and communicate them to employees.

DID YOU:

_____ Write guidelines in clear, understandable language?
_____ Incorporate a progressive system into your guidelines?
_____ Fit punishment to the infraction and the safe and efficient operation of the foodservice?
_____ Include in your guidelines an appeal procedure?
_____ Include in your guidelines conditions for removing past disciplinary notices?
_____ Communicate your guidelines to new and current employees?

PERFORMANCE MANAGEMENT SKILLS CHECKLIST Continued

19. Handle counterproductive behaviors using a two-step process.

DID YOU:

_____ Do a thorough investigation in a timely manner before drawing any conclusions?

_____ Before taking any corrective action, examine the evidence, any extenuating circumstances, the employee's understanding of the rules, the employee's past performance, the seriousness of the problem, and past practice?

_____ Act in a fair and consistent manner?

_____ Show support and express concern to your employees?

_____ Maintain the self-respect and self-esteem of the employee?

_____ Use corrective action in a timely manner?

_____ Document the performance as soon as possible?

_____ Make sure your documentation was specific, behavior-oriented, accurate, thorough, and objective?

_____ Document the corrective action taken, the employee's plan for improvement, and follow-up date?

_____ Clearly tell the employee what the next step in the disciplinary process will be if things don't improve?

_____ Explain the appeals process to the employee and invite him or her to write down any comments?

20. Prevent counterproductive behaviors.

DID YOU:

_____ Hire the right people?

_____ Effectively manage performance?

_____ Carefully select supervisors with good human relations skills?

_____ Listen actively to your employees and try to understand their needs?

4

Employees Want to Be Rewarded

21. Reward your employees.
22. Follow employee reward guidelines.
23. Pay for performance.
24. Institute a profit-sharing or other gain-sharing program for employees.

Employees feel commitment when they believe that someone recognizes and rewards their efforts, especially when that someone is their boss. They tend to feel a greater commitment when reward is tied to job performance. When an employee is rewarded for his or her own abilities or achievements, it is infinitely more satisfying than being rewarded for seniority or for meeting a criterion that everyone meets, regardless of ability to perform. Recognition of employees' contributions is of utmost importance in keeping them on board. Keep in mind that you can never give too much praise or say too many thank-yous.

This chapter will cover traditional rewards, such as praise and bonuses, and nontraditional reward systems, such as pay for performance and gain-sharing plans. Other nontraditional rewards, information sharing with employees and employee involvement programs, were discussed in Chapter 2.

21. Reward Your Employees

What can you reward your employees for? Here are just a few of many deserving behaviors and contributions.

- Meeting or exceeding performance standards
- Performance above and beyond job duties

- Attaining sales goals or profitability goals
- Serving a predetermined number of covers
- Selling a predetermined number of specific menu items such as appetizers, wines, or desserts
- Having good attendance
- Being with the foodservice for five or more years
- Completing training
- Working as a team member
- Reducing the number of accidents
- Making a suggestion that is successfully implemented

Once you have determined when to recognize employees, you need to think about how to reward them. Rewards can range from verbal praise to material awards such as cash bonuses or free vacations. Here are some examples of rewards.

- Verbal praise
- Certificate or plaque (see Figs. 4-1 and 4-2)
- Announcement in newsletter or on bulletin board (with photo)
- Memos and letters (see Fig. 3-3)
- Service pin
- Article of clothing, perhaps with company logo on it
- Cash bonus
- Merchandise
- Gift certificate or gift selected from a catalog
- Free or reduced-price meal(s)
- Free tickets to sports events, concerts
- Chances to win a prize
- Points toward prizes
- Vacation trips
- Celebration party
- Time off with pay
- Larger or nicer office
- Special parking spot
- Special job title
- More responsibility
- Assignment to a committee
- Training/professional education
- Promotion

Several of these rewards will now be discussed in more detail. Frequent, sincere verbal praise can work wonders in any foodservice operation. Praise can be used to reinforce and shape employees'

Fig. 4-1 25 TYPES OF CERTIFICATES

Certificate of Training
Certificate of Completion
Certificate of Achievement
Certificate of Appreciation
Certificate of Attendance
Certificate of Promotion
Certificate of Service Excellence
Certificate of Sales Achievement
Certificate of Participation
Certificate of Outstanding Performance
Certificate of Long-Term Service (5, 10, 15, 20, 25 years)
Certificate of Outstanding Safety Practices
Certificate of Outstanding Sanitation Practices
Certificate of Leadership
Safe Driver Award
Best Suggestion Award
Team Player Award
Team Leader Award
Better Idea Award
Endurance Award
Dedicated Service Award
Customer Satisfaction Award
Most Valuable Player Award
Employee of the Month
Employee of the Year
Employee of the Moment

Fig. 4-2 EMPLOYEE CERTIFICATE

Congratulations

Certificate of Completion

This Certificate Is Given to:

____

on ______________________________

for Successfully Completing

Training in ______________________

____

____

by ______________________________

knowledge, skills, or attitudes. Public praise for accomplishments and contributions is especially effective. For at least 10 minutes each day do nothing but work on catching your employees doing things right, and then use these steps.

1. Describe the specific action you are praising.
2. Explain the results or effects of the action.
3. State your appreciation.
4. Ask the employee how he or she feels about doing a good job.
5. Say thank you.
6. Write a letter of thanks and make sure a copy goes into the employee's personnel file.

Bonuses are one-time or periodic payments given in addition to the basic wage to reward employees for extra work performed. They may be given for individual or group effort. Some restaurants use sales figures, cover counts, or simple managerial judgment to determine bonuses for employees in almost all job categories. Hourly employees of Long John Silver's are entitled to a prorated cash bonus of up to 10 percent of gross pay each quarter if their restaurant's sales and profits are higher than those of the previous year. In another restaurant, if the number of meals served in the dining room surpasses a certain number, the kitchen staff receives bonus hours of pay; servers who exceed the average sales for a shift also receive bonuses.

Have an "Employee of the Month," "Hero of the Month," or "Employee of the Moment" award. To make the program credible, it is important to establish criteria (see Fig. 4-3), which may be developed from the vision statement and guiding principles. Publicize the awards; for example, post the winners' pictures in service areas. Use company social events to announce awards, such as for "Employee of the Month."

22. Follow Employee Reward Guidelines

Here is a list of suggestions on how to get the most from your employee reward programs.

- Whenever possible, recognize and reward employees publicly. This makes the recipients feel great, encourages others to strive for recognition, and reinforces the values and goals of the company.
- Always give recognition in a positive and sincere manner.

Fig. 4-3 CRITERIA FOR EMPLOYEE OF THE MONTH PROGRAM

EMPLOYEE OF THE MONTH PROGRAM

The Employee of the Month is chosen using a weighted point program. Circle the number of points in each category to which the employee is entitled, and total them up. Maximum number of points is 100.

Month of: ____________________

Employee's Name and Title: ____________________

Employee's Supervisor: ____________________

1. Job Performance
   - Meets or exceeds job standards 95% of the time. — 25 points
   - Meets or exceeds job standards 80% of the time. — 20 points
   - Meets or exceeds job standards less than 80% of the time. — 15 points
2. Gets Along Well With Others
   - Does an outstanding job of being friendly and helpful to others. — 25 points
   - Does a good job of being friendly and helpful to others. — 20 points
   - Does a satisfactory job of being friendly and helpful to others. — 15 points
3. Follows Policies and Procedures
   - Follows policies and procedures without incident — 15 points
   - Follows policies and procedures with one incident — 10 points
   - Follows policies and procedures with two incidents — 5 points
4. Attendance
   - No absences or latenesses — 15 points
   - One absence or lateness — 10 points
   - Two absences and/or latenesses — 5 points
5. Attends Meetings and Training Sessions
   - Attended all relevant meetings and training session — 20 points
   - Attended all but one meeting or training session — 15 points

TOTAL POINTS: ____________

- When having a contest, do not pit employees against one another in an attempt to win only one or a few prizes. When only a few people can win, most employees do not even try. They are disheartened, rather than motivated, when the winner(s) is announced. Instead, make it possible for all employees to win in a contest. Have individuals compete with themselves to beat their own individual goals, rather than compete with peers.
- Do not recognize only your superb performers. About 10 percent of your employees are top-notch workers, who you pray will never leave. If you recognize only these performers, you will frustrate the majority of your employees who are not only satisfactory performers, but the backbone of your operation. In addition to the heros, champion the average employees who come to work on time, follow rules, work safely, and so forth.
- Determine which employees will be recognized by using objective criteria. In this manner, you will be less likely to make decisions based on favoritism, seniority, or pity.
- Recognize employees in a timely fashion. Do not make your recognition program so complicated and unwieldy that it takes too long to make announcements and hand out awards or prizes.
- From time to time, recognize employees when they least expect it; be somewhat unpredictable. For example, tell an individual to take the rest of the day off.
- Rewards should be tied to true accomplishments, not to superficial or momentary gains.
- Rewards should be of appropriate value. Small rewards can be just as impressive as large ones.
- A reward should be something desired by your employees. Ask them what types of rewards they prefer.

23. Pay for Performance

Pay for performance refers to a system of paying employees according to how well they perform their jobs. Merit raises, a system of giving pay increases to employees based on job performance, constitute the most popular pay-for-performance method. Studies of both executives and employees show that when pay is tied to performance, satisfaction, motivation, and productivity increase. For many people, increased pay lifts self-esteem, pride, and prestige.

The use of merit raises will fail to serve its motivational purpose under certain conditions:

- If the employees do not understand and accept the system
- If employees do not trust the managers who make decisions that affect their merit raises
- If managers base their decisions on favoritism, seniority, or pity
- If employees can successfully pressure their supervisors to give them a greater increase

Table 4-1 gives an example of merit guidelines. Depending on the employee's rating and his or her position in the wage range within a particular class, wages increase by a certain percentage. In some cases, the raise is given in a single amount, called a lump-sum payment; this is often given to employees who are "red-circled," which means that their wage rate has reached the maximum for their grade.

Related to pay for performance is *pay for knowledge*. Pay for knowledge refers to a system in which pay is determined by the number of jobs an employee can do, not by the job the employee actually does on any specific day. This type of system is seen most often in fast-food establishments that use a team or crew concept. The largest franchisee of Arby's awards employees a progression of bronze, silver, and gold name tags, as well as pay increases, as they learn each area of the store. When all areas have been learned, the employee is promoted to the position of crew leader.

The advantages of a pay for knowledge system include making work challenging, giving employees a broader perspective, giving management more flexibility in scheduling employees, and enhancing customer responsiveness. A major disadvantage is the higher training costs.

24. Institute a Profit-Sharing or Other Gain-Sharing Program for Employees

Profit sharing is the most popular type of gain-sharing plan. A gain-sharing plan is a group incentive plan designed to enhance retention and recruitment, as well as high levels of productivity, through sharing the financial gains (profits) of the organization with its employees. For gain-sharing to be most effective, employees need to have realistic opportunities to influence profits. Gain-sharing also works best with a merit pay or pay for knowledge system.

There are basically three types of profit-sharing programs. In a cash plan, the profits are distributed annually or quarterly. In a deferred plan, there is no significant payment until retirement, disability, or severance. Deferred plans are the most popular, because the employee

Table 4-1 Merit Guidelines

	*Amount of Raise (%), Based on Employee's Position in the Wage Range**			
Performance Rating	*Below 25%*	*Below 50%*	*Below 75%*	*Below 90%*
Outstanding	15	12	9	6
Good	13	10	7	4
Meets standards	10	7	4	2
Below standards	No raise until performance is brought up to at least "Meets standards."			
Unsatisfactory				

*If the current wage is between 90 and 99 percent of the wage range, the increase will be to the maximum of the range. For employees who are already at the top of the wage range, a lump sum will be paid.

can defer the tax on the income. Some plans, referred to as combined plans, include both cash and deferred payments. Often employees become eligible to participate in profit sharing upon reaching 21 years of age and having worked 1,000 hours.

In a 1985 study for the National Restaurant Association, 17 percent of restaurants surveyed were shown to have a form of profit sharing, a figure lower than was found in manufacturing (25 percent) and retail and wholesale (33 percent).

Other examples of gain-sharing programs that aim to increase employee satisfaction and job performance, and decrease turnover, include stock ownership plans and 401(k) plans. Employee stock ownership plans (ESOPs) are more often used by larger foodservice companies to encourage employee purchase of company stock, which is usually offered at a reduced price.

Using 401(k) plans, named after section 401(k) of the Internal Revenue Code, employees can save for retirement through payroll deductions, which are not taxed, and possibly have their savings matched by their employer. In most 401(k) plans, full vesting occurs immediately or within 5 years, which means that the employee has a right to the pension should he or she leave the company. The 1986 Tax Reform Act limits the salary deferral to $7,000, which will rise slightly as the cost of living increases.

ASSESSMENT OF REWARDING SKILLS

Directions: In the blank space at the front of each item, put the number which best indicates your estimation of the frequency of each behavior.

Scale: 5—Never, 4—Seldom, 3—Occasionally, 2—Usually, 1—Always

_____ 21. Reward your employees.
_____ 22. Follow employee reward guidelines.

The more frequently you use the above behaviors, the better you are at rewarding your employees. In any case where you gave yourself a "3" or higher, use the following checklist to work harder on these skills.

REWARDING SKILLS CHECKLIST

Directions: Use this checklist at periodic intervals, such as every month, to see how well you are doing in the selected skill areas. Check off the skills you used, as a way to reinforce your positive behaviors, and circle those skills you have not used but wish to. Keep this checklist handy as a reminder of the skills you want to work on.

21. Reward your employees.

DID YOU:

_____ Take at least 10 minutes each day to do nothing but praise your employees for doing something right?

_____ Put a letter of thanks into one or more employee's files?

_____ Take part in a reward program, such as helping determine the recipient of an "Employee of the Month" program or designing a new bonus program?

22. Follow employee reward guidelines.

DID YOU:

_____ Recognize and reward employees publicly?

_____ Recognize the satisfactory, as well as the outstanding, performers?

_____ When having a contest, have individuals compete with themselves rather than with a peer?

_____ Recognize employees without regard to favoritism, popularity, seniority, or pity?

_____ Recognize employees in a timely fashion?

_____ Surprise someone with a reward?

_____ Tie rewards to true accomplishments?

_____ Make rewards of appropriate value?

_____ Make sure the rewards offered were those desired by the employees?

5

Employees Want to Do Interesting, Important, and Challenging Work

25. Help employees see the end result of their work.
26. Let your employees make as many of their own decisions as possible.
27. Cross-train employees and rotate their positions.
28. Give employees special assignments.
29. Have a career ladder and promote from within.
30. Offer employees opportunities for personal and professional development.
31. Bring in people from the community for tours and cooking classes.

When work is interesting and has some importance, employees can feel their jobs are worthwhile. Most employees also want to be challenged on the job. This chapter will discuss seven ways to provide interesting, important, and challenging foodservice jobs.

25. Help Employees See the End Result of Their Work

One way to keep work important and interesting to your employees is to make sure that they see the end result of what they do. Employees who work directly with guests are naturally able to see the satisfied guests and hear the compliments (as well as the complaints). Yet how many times do your cooks see satisfied guests or hear their compliments? Probably rarely. How many times do your dishwashers get to see how attractive the tables look supplied with their clean wares? What can you do to help your employees see the end result of their work? For kitchen employees who are not normally able to see guests, try one of these ideas.

- Hang pictures in the kitchen of some of your guests, famous or otherwise, enjoying a meal.
- Ask kitchen employees to walk periodically through the dining area with you to speak with guests.
- Post any complimentary letters from guests after you have read them to your employees.
- Ask guests to walk through the kitchen and introduce them to your employees.
- Recently, some operators have made a table in the kitchen available for guests as a result of guests' interest in seeing the kitchen staff perform their cooking duties. In most restaurants, this table is booked far in advance. Other operators have built kitchens with glass windows so guests can watch their meals being prepared.

26. Let Your Employees Make as Many of Their Own Decisions as Possible

Probably the most effective way to empower your employees is to let them make as many of their own decisions as possible. For example, dining room employees can be empowered to handle customer complaints the way they think best. One company that operates fine-dining restaurants in the Northwest found this system to have wonderful results. Instead of having to fill out forms, ask the guest questions, and speak with a supervisor, the dining room employees (even dining room attendants) were allowed to do what they thought was needed to keep the customer happy. This might involve offering a free dessert or a free dinner, or another course of action. Of course, employees were given some guidelines but still had to use their own discretion. The company's president, Timothy W. Firnstahl,* reported:

> In the beginning, employees were wary of their new authority. . . . But once they got used to the idea, employees liked knowing that the

*Timothy W. Firnstahl, Service With a Smile—And a Guarantee, *Restaurants USA*, April, 1990, p. 16.

> company believed so strongly in its products and services that it wholeheartedly stood behind its work—and theirs. Preeminence in any field gives people feelings of self-worth they can never get from just making a buck. Their power as company representatives increased their pride in the business, and that, in turn, increased motivation.

There are other areas in which you may want to give employees more latitude in decision making. Consider doing the following:

- Ask the cooks to take responsibility for checking the quality of all foods served.
- Allow the storekeeper to adjust delivery invoices.
- Ask the dishwasher to determine when to take a break, as long as it is during a slow time.

27. Cross-Train Employees and Rotate Their Positions

Cross-training employees benefits management as much as, if not more than, it benefits employees. You can start a cross-training program by following these five steps.

1. List the major tasks of employees in each functional work area, such as hot food production or sanitation/cleaning.
2. List the employees in each area, and which tasks each can perform. These employees may be able to cross-train each other on what they already know.
3. List the tasks each employee needs to be trained on. These represent your training needs.
4. Make a training schedule for each person, including what he or she will be trained in and how long it will take. Always cross-train first on skills that only one or two people can now perform.
5. Support your cross-training efforts by making sure your schedule is adhered to and rewarding trainers and trainees.

Once a sufficient number of employees are cross-trained in a given area, they can be rotated through the different positions to provide them variety and interest. A common example of cross-training in the foodservice industry is seen in many fast-food restaurants. Hourly employees are gradually trained to do the jobs of any crew member, including cooking, cashiering, cleaning, and so on.

28. Give Employees Special Assignments

As a challenge, you can assign employees special assignments or projects. The nature of assignments will depend on the employee's position and his or her interests and ambitions. For instance, a cook may want to help the storekeeper to reorganize the freezer so that everyone can find things more easily. Make sure that the employee wants to carry out the special assignment, and that you give recognition when it is completed.

29. Have a Career Ladder and Promote from Within

Any operator can set up a career ladder by which an employee can be promoted in steps to higher-level jobs, each requiring more skills and entailing greater responsibility. Generally, the progression of jobs is evident in the operator's chain of command. For instance, in a fast-food restaurant, a crew member may aspire to become an assistant manager, and then the unit manager. In a full-service restaurant, a busperson may work toward being a server, and then on to dining room supervisor and, eventually, management trainee.

Guidelines for Making a Career Ladder Work

- Set up the career ladder. A good resource to consider is your organizational chart. You may want to have a career ladder for all staff, or for just one part of the operation, such as the cooking area. See Fig. 5-1 for examples.
- Management needs to set clear criteria for promotion. Criteria may include a minimum level of performance on past evaluations and a minimum amount of time on the current job. Criteria for each position should be identified and communicated to all employees, along with a promote-from-within policy statement.
- Management must be completely committed in words and actions to the plan and consider it a long-term investment. Of course, within any operation there are times when hiring an outsider is more desirable than promoting from within, such as when a new perspective and ideas are needed. In such a case, it is important to communicate this rationale to employees who were not promoted.
- Criteria for promotion must be adhered to consistently at all times. If they are relaxed for any individual, the credibility of the program will be diminished.
- Employees must be promoted in a consistent and fair manner. Favoritism has no place in promotion.

Fig. 5-1 CAREER LADDER

- When employees are promoted, provide tangible rewards and increased pay. Again, be consistent with your rewards and pay.
- Do not be surprised or disappointed when someone you have promoted does not work out. This will happen from time to time and does not necessarily mean the system is not valid.
- It is important to recognize that not everyone wants promotion or is promotable. Do not put pressure on a person who is happy where he or she is.

30. Offer Employees Opportunities for Personal and Professional Development

In addition to the usual job skills training, why not offer employees an opportunity to take classes to develop personal and/or professional skills? You might offer on-site classes or reimbursement for classes taken at local community colleges or other sites. Employees could work on developing personal skills such as:

Maintaining a positive attitude
Managing stress
Building a healthy self-image
Financial planning
Developing good habits in fitness and nutrition
Being a good parent
Acquiring basic literacy skills

Professional skills that an employee may wish to work on might include any of the following:

Human relations skills
Communication skills

Supervisory skills
Foodservice operations skills

You can also make printed materials available to employees, such as foodservice trade magazines, foodservice books, self-study courses (see Appendix C), product literature, and booklets or brochures on a variety of personal or health-related topics, such as AIDS.

To further challenge and develop your employees, why not take several to a local industry trade show or association meeting? Besides being an educational experience, this kind of field trip can enhance your employees' pride in what they do.

31. Bring In People from the Community for Tours and Cooking Classes

A great way to show your employees the importance of their jobs is to invite various groups, such as school children or hospitality management college students, to tour your operation. Another way to instill self-confidence and pride is to ask members of your cooking staff if they would like to lead cooking classes for interested community members. Ask your employees to help give the tour, for example, by demonstrating cooking techniques.

ASSESSMENT OF EMPLOYEE DEVELOPMENT SKILLS

Directions: In the blank space at the front of each item, put the number which best indicates your estimation of the frequency of each behavior.

Scale: 5—Never, 4—Seldom, 3—Occasionally, 2—Usually, 1—Always

_____ 25. Help employees see the end result of their work.

_____ 26. Let your employees make as many of their own decisions as possible.

_____ 27. Cross-train employees and rotate their positions.

_____ 28. Give employees special assignments.

_____ 29. Use a career ladder to promote from within.

_____ 30. Offer employees opportunities for personal and professional development.

_____ 31. Bring in people from the community for tours and cooking classes.

The more frequently you use the above behaviors, the better you are at developing your employees. In any case where you gave yourself a "3" or higher, use the following Checklist to work harder on these skills.

EMPLOYEE DEVELOPMENT SKILLS CHECKLIST

Directions: Use this checklist at periodic intervals, such as every month, to see how well you are doing in the selected skill areas. Check off the actions you took, as a way to reinforce your positive behaviors, and circle those you have not taken but wish to. Keep this checklist handy as a reminder of the skills you want to work on.

25. Help employees see the end result of their work.

DID YOU:

_____ Hang pictures in the kitchen of some of your guests, famous or otherwise, enjoying a meal?
_____ Ask kitchen employees to accompany you as you greet the guests?
_____ Read aloud and post all complimentary letters from guests?
_____ Ask guests to come into your kitchen and introduce your employees?
_____ (Describe something you did.) ____________________

---

26. Let your employees make as many of their own decisions as possible.

DID YOU:

_____ Ask your servers to personally handle all guest complaints on-the-spot?
_____ (Describe something you did.) ____________________

---

27. Cross-train employees and rotate their positions.

DID YOU:

_____ Set up a training schedule for each person, including what he or she will be trained in and how long it will take?
_____ Make sure your training schedule was adhered to?
_____ Reward your trainers and trainees?

EMPLOYEE DEVELOPMENT SKILLS CHECKLIST Continued

28. Give employees special assignments.

DID YOU:

_____ Make sure the employee is capable of carrying out the special assignment?
_____ Make sure the employee wanted to carry out the special assignment?
_____ Give recognition to the employee when the task was completed?
_____ (Describe something you assigned) ________________________

____

____

29. Use a career ladder to promote from within.

DID YOU:

_____ Set up a career ladder?
_____ Clearly set criteria for promotion?
_____ Adhere to the criteria for promotion consistently?
_____ Promote in a consistent and fair manner?
_____ Provide tangible reward and increased pay?

30. Offer employees opportunities for personal and professional development.

DID YOU:

_____ Offer employees the opportunity to take classes to develop personal skills?
_____ Offer employees the opportunity to take classes to develop professional skills?
_____ Make available to employees printed materials and self-study courses to promote professional development?
_____ Take one or more of your employees to a trade show or industry meeting?

EMPLOYEE DEVELOPMENT SKILLS CHECKLIST Continued

31. Bring in people from the community for tours and cooking classes.

    DID YOU:

    _____ Invite groups such as school children or high school students to come in for a tour?

    _____ Invite local community members to come for cooking classes?

    _____ Ask one (or more) of your employees to give a tour?

    _____ Ask one (or more) of your employees to teach cooking?

6

Employees Want Managers Who Know What They Are Doing and Who Are Good Role Models

32. Be able to perform the jobs you supervise.
33. Manage your time.
34. Be visible.
35. Be a good role model.

When employees work for an incompetent manager, it seems there is always an atmosphere of crisis that constantly demands extra efforts. Before long the stress level becomes overwhelming and employees start to leave. Employees want their boss to respect them; likewise, they want to be able to respect their boss.

32. Be Able to Perform the Jobs You Supervise

When a new foodservice manager starts a job, the employees always test to see what the new person knows and whether he or she knows the area well. It is important, to both the employees and the operation, that you be able to perform the jobs you supervise and know their technical aspects. This gives employees the assurance that you can understand their needs and frustrations and evaluate their performance accurately.

At times you may feel you need to learn something more about an aspect of foodservice in order to do your job better. Appendix C lists sources of self-study foodservice courses that can help you learn more about many aspects of foodservice.

33. Manage Your Time

To appear confident in what you are doing, you cannot be racing about from one thing to another. Although foodservice managers are interrupted an average of once every 7 to 8 minutes and probably have good reason to feel panicky at times, employees need, want, and respect a boss who is calm, cool, and in control at all times.

There are time-management principles and techniques available to help managers gain control of their time, their jobs, and their lives.

To manage your time better, first plan your work and set priorities. Each day make a "to do" list, preferably in a calendar, noting all appointments, and refer to it frequently to stay focused. Rank each item by establishing A, B, and C priorities. Most time should be spent on A priorities, which are the most important, then in order, B priorities are of medium importance, and C priorities are of low importance. If in doubt about the importance of a task, ask yourself, "What would happen if I did not do this?" Plan the day, but leave time for unexpected situations, interruptions, and relaxation. Try to set aside uninterrupted blocks of time for work on more complex tasks and let people know you do not wish to be interrupted during this time.

While working, keep on track. Consider frequently during the day, "What is the best use of my time right now?" Do not procrastinate. Do the disliked jobs first, because they are the tasks most likely to be put off indefinitely. Divide large jobs into smaller parts, so that you can get started and keep moving.

Keep socializing to a minimum. Ask friends and family to call at work only if there is an emergency. If possible, have someone else answer the telephone. Plan to return phone calls at a certain time each day. Avoid calling people at lunchtime, when they are likely to be away from their desks. Do not hesitate to have phone calls held while you are doing something important or when concentration is necessary. Get to the point with callers, and tell long-winded ones that you must attend a meeting right away. To cut down on visitors dropping in, ask people to make appointments in advance. If you have established this as policy, do not break your rule by allowing casual visitors into the office when they show up saying, "I was in the area so I thought I would drop in."

To cut down on the number of peers and employees who drop into the office, close the door when necessary. When someone does come in, stand up and remain standing until the person has said what he or she has to say—this can help to speed the visit. Ask employees not to come to you with every problem and question as it occurs, but rather to save several issues to discuss at one time. Ask them to offer solutions instead of questions. To reduce the likelihood of frequent interruptions, make sure your desk is located away from the view of others.

It is important to learn to delegate work. Do not waste time doing a task that someone else would like to do and can do as well—or better. Delegation is a wonderful way to develop employees and allow you more time to manage. Effective delegation does not mean telling someone what to do, but rather mutually discussing and agreeing on a plan of action. Both parties should agree on what is to be accomplished and how it is to be monitored and evaluated.

Organize your work area and handle paperwork efficiently (see Fig 6-1). For good organization, use boxes or trays labeled In, Out, Action, Pending, Read, and File. Under the desk should be the most important file: the wastebasket. All papers should be handled once and put into their appropriate places. When letters or notes arrive, handwrite an answer directly on them and mail them back to their senders. Use a tape recorder to dictate letters and memos. Carry a pad at all times to jot down ideas and things that must be done. Keep the desk clear of everything except the current task.

Fig. 6-1 ORGANIZED DESK

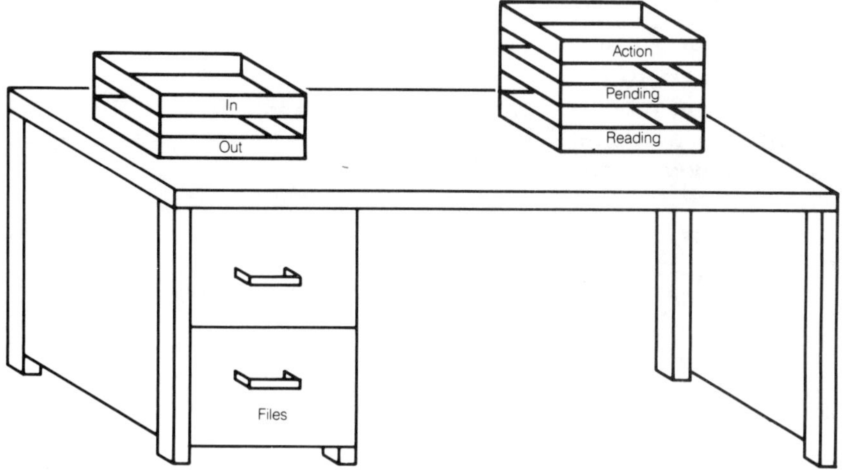

Decide to be decisive. Make decisions, and act promptly.

Find time for non-work-related activities because they are essential to recharging your batteries and having a refreshed outlook. Exercise, relax, spend time with friends and family, and participate in other activities you enjoy.

In summary, do the following:

- Keep a sense of what is important. Ask yourself, will this matter in 5 years?
- Take action. It keeps you feeling good about yourself.
- Have a support system to count on as a buffer and revitalizer.

Many times the difference between success and failure in business is explained by one short sentence: "I did not have the time."

34. Be Visible

Being visible to your employees is important when its purpose is to show concern and caring about your operation and employees. If your idea of being visible is to hover over people so you can pounce on them whenever they make a mistake, they will wish you were invisible. If, on the other hand, you prefer to stay in your office and avoid your troops as much as possible, employees will feel that you do not really know what is going on. You will gain your employees' respect by being visible, knowledgable, and involved.

35. Be a Good Role Model

Like it or not, you are a role model for your employees. If you do not work hard, get to work on time, and wear appropriate clothes, you cannot expect your employees to. Employees take their cue from you, the boss. As a role model, you set standards for employees. To be a good role model, you need to do the following:

- Come to work on time every day and call in sick only when absolutely necessary. Come back from breaks on time or early.
- Follow established procedures and rules. If you do not, neither will your employees.
- Apply procedures and rules equitably to everyone.
- Make sure someone always knows where you are.
- Be friendly. Spend time every day talking with each of your employees.

Have a positive attitude toward your job and show your enthusiasm. This is crucial to establishing a pleasant work climate.

Never poke fun at or berate your boss to your employees, unless you would like them to do the same to you.

Be neat and well organized.

Be assertive. Being assertive means that you communicate your positive and negative feelings honestly and directly, and, at the same time, respect and try to understand the other person's position. Be being assertive you demonstrate self-respect and self-confidence as well as awareness of and respect for the rights of others. Your employees will be more likely to express their ideas and concerns if you do so.

Listen sincerely to your employees.

Stay calm at all times. Leave any moodiness at home.

Be honest and forthright with your employees. If you are ever dishonest, you will lose their trust and respect.

Keep any promises made to employees.

When you make a mistake, admit it. Your employees will appreciate your honesty and realize that you are human too. They will also be more likely to discuss their mistakes openly with you. Also, acknowledge not knowing all the answers.

Show respect, trust, and caring toward everyone.

Maintain a sense of humor. Everyone likes to have fun at work, so why not set the tone for an enjoyable workplace?

Recognize your employees' efforts and give credit where credit is due.

Be consistent in what you do and how you act.

To be a perfect role model all the time may not be possible, but it is a worthwhile objective.

ASSESSMENT OF BASIC SKILLS

Directions: In the blank space at the front of each item, put the number which best indicates your estimation of the frequency of each behavior.

Scale: 5—Never, 4—Seldom, 3—Occasionally, 2—Usually, 1—Always

_____ 32. Be able to perform the jobs you supervise.
_____ 33. Manage your time.
_____ 34. Be visible.
_____ 35. Be a good role model.

The more frequently you use the above behaviors, the better you are at basic skills. In any case where you gave yourself a "3" or higher, use the following Checklist to work harder on these skills.

BASIC SKILLS CHECKLIST

Directions: Use this checklist at periodic intervals, such as every month, to see how well you are doing in the selected skill areas. Check off the skills you used, as a way to reinforce your positive behaviors, and circle those skills you have not used but wish to. Keep this checklist handy as a reminder of the skills you want to work on.

32. Be able to perform the jobs you supervise.

DID YOU:

_____ Feel as though you could do the jobs you supervise if you had to in an emergency?

List any jobs here you want to learn more about:

____

____

33. Manage your time.

DID YOU:

_____ Make a "to do" list and set priorities?
_____ Use your "to do" list to stay focused?
_____ Set aside blocks of time when you let everyone know you did not want to be interrupted?
_____ Do the disliked jobs first?
_____ Keep socializing to a minimum?
_____ Ask drop-in visitors to make appointments?
_____ Return phone calls at a certain time each day?
_____ Close the door of your office when necessary?
_____ Get to the point with phone and other conversations?
_____ Delegate some jobs?
_____ Organize your work area (boxes for in, out, action, pending, read, file, and a big garbage can)?
_____ Handle papers only once?
_____ Dictate correspondence?
_____ Carry a pad at all times?

BASIC SKILLS CHECKLIST Continued

_____ Keep your desk clear except for the current task?
_____ Decide to be decisive?
_____ Keep a sense of what is important?
_____ Find time for non-work-related activities?

34. Be visible.

DID YOU:

_____ Spend more time walking around the operation than sitting in your office?
_____ Talk to employees as you were walking around?

35. Be a good role model.

DID YOU:

_____ Come to work on time and call in sick only when absolutely necessary?
_____ Follow all other rules?
_____ Make sure someone always knew where you were?
_____ Act friendly?
_____ Have a positive attitude and show enthusiasm?
_____ Always say positive things about your boss?
_____ Have everything well-organized?
_____ Sincerely listen to your employees?
_____ Stay calm at all times?
_____ Act honestly with employees?
_____ Keep any promises made to your employees?
_____ Admit when you made a mistake?
_____ Show respect, trust, and caring toward everyone?
_____ Keep a sense of humor?
_____ Act consistently?
_____ Act assertively?

7

Employees Want Good Pay, Benefits, and Working Conditions

36. Establish competitive and equitable pay rates.
37. Offer a competitive benefit package suited to your employees.
38. Provide a reasonable work schedule.
39. Provide a pleasant, safe, and clean work environment.
40. Have fun while you work.

Compensating your employees fairly and providing good working conditions are basic requirements in any industry. Although dissatisfaction with pay, benefits, or working conditions is rarely the only reason an employee leaves, it may, along with other complaints, cause an employee to look elsewhere for work.

36. Establish Competitive and Equitable Pay Rates

Any compensation system should be competitive with those of other local employers so as to attract and to retain, employees. The best way to determine what your competition is offering is to conduct a wage survey once a year or every other year, depending on competition and inflation. By obtaining wage information from organizations that compete for the same personnel you need, you are able to offer employees wages that are equivalent to—or better than—those paid at other establishments.

To conduct a wage survey, you need first to identify key jobs for comparison with the same or similar positions elsewhere. Key jobs, also called benchmark jobs, are recognized as such by other foodservices and vary little from operation to operation. Examples include dishwasher, server, dining room attendant, cashier, and entry-level cook. Next, select 10 to 15 area employers who are representative of the various types of establishments—large and small, new and established—against which you compete.

The next task is to develop survey questions, being specific about the necessary type of data (wages, benefits, compensation policy), degree of detail (hourly, daily, weekly, or monthly), and degree of experience (new employees, those in midcareer, or long-term employees). Figure 7-1 depicts a sample Wage and Benefits Survey form.

When doing the survey, either by phone or mail, be sure you are comparing like jobs by having available the key points of each job description and the job qualifications.

Another source of information about hourly wages and benefits is available from the National Restaurant Association. In its *1990 Survey of Wages for Hourly Employees,* information from over 6,300 participating foodservice operators is tabulated. Median hourly wages for various employees are shown in Table 7-1. Survey results report wages on a regional, state, and, in some cases, substate basis. They are available by calling the National Restaurant Association at 1-800-424-5156.

37. Offer a Competitive Benefit Package Suited to Your Employees

Benefits were originally referred to as "fringe benefits" because, at the time they were instituted, they were quite meager and given in addition to a paycheck. The scope and costs of benefits have expanded widely. Employee benefit costs have greatly affected business expenses and profits since enactment of the first workers' state compensation law (in about 1900) and passage of the Social Security Act of 1935. An average benefit cost for an American company is 36 percent of payroll, although median benefit costs for hourly foodservice workers are 18 percent of payroll. While few cost changes are expected for benefits such as life insurance, disability, and time off, health insurance costs have been skyrocketing, and such programs may be made mandatory at some point by the federal government.

A benefits program should meet objectives set by the operator, such as attracting and retaining employees, meeting employee health and security needs, and increasing employee morale, motivation, growth,

Fig. 7-1 WAGE AND BENEFITS SURVEY FORM

WAGE AND BENEFITS SURVEY

Date: ____________________

Name of Operation: ____

Location: ____

Contact: ____

PROFILE

Type of restaurant: _____ Full-menu tableservice
_____ Limited-menu tableservice
_____ Limited-menu, no tableservice
_____ Cafeteria

Number of establishments: _______

Foodservice Contract _______ Franchise Operation _______

Number of hourly employees at this location: _______

Union _______ Non-Union _______

Annual sales volume: _____ Under $499,999
_____ $500,000 to $999,999
_____ $1,000,000 to $1,499,999
_____ $1,500,000 to $4,999,999
_____ Over $5,000,000

Fig. 7-1 Continued

WAGE SURVEY

How often are employees able to get a wage increase? ____________________

Position/Title	No. of Employees	Starting Wage	Maximum Wage
Cook			
Assistant cook			
Short-order cook			
Baker			
Food/salad preparation worker			
Crew person (fast food)			
Crew supervisor (fast food)			
Cafeteria server			
Waiter/waitress			
Host/hostess			
Bartender			
Cashier			
Busperson			
Dishwasher			
Janitor/porter			
Delivery driver			

Fig. 7-1 Continued

BENEFITS SURVEY

DO YOU OFFER:	YES	NO
MEDICAL/SURGICAL INSURANCE	______	______
Who's eligible? ______		
Who pays what? ______		
PRESCRIPTION PLAN	______	______
Who's eligible? ______		
Amount of copayment ______		
DENTAL INSURANCE	______	______
Who's eligible? ______		
Who pays what? ______		
VISION INSURANCE	______	______
Who's eligible? ______		
Who pays what? ______		
LIFE INSURANCE	______	______
Amount ______		
Who's eligible? ______		
Who pays what? ______		
PENSION/CAPITAL-ACCUMULATION PLANS	______	______
Who's eligible? ______		
Who pays what? ______		
Details ______		
______		
FREE MEALS	______	______
UNIFORMS PROVIDED	______	______

Fig. 7-1 Continued

DO YOU OFFER:	YES	NO
UNIFORMS CLEANED	______	______
VACATION	______	______
Who's eligible? ______		
Amount ______		
______		
SICK PAY	______	______
Who's eligible? ______		
How much? ______		
HOLIDAY PAY	______	______
Who's eligible? ______		
How much? ______		
BONUSES/AWARDS	______	______
How do they work? ______		
______		
EDUCATIONAL ASSISTANCE	______	______
Who's eligible? ______		
Percent reimbursement ______		
What courses are eligible? ______		
ANY OTHER NOTEWORTHY BENEFITS? ______	______	______
______		
______		
______		
______		

Table 7-1 1990 Hourly Wages for Hourly Foodservice Employees

Type of Hourly Employee	*Median Hourly Wage*
Cook	$6.50
Assistant Cook	5.80
Short-order cook	5.75
Baker	6.25
Food/salad preparation worker	5.25
Crew person (fast-food)	4.25
Crew supervisor (fast-food)	5.55
Cafeteria server	4.88
Waiter/waitress	2.60
Host/hostess	5.00
Bartender	5.00
Cashier	5.00
Busperson	4.00
Dishwasher	4.50
Janitor/porter	5.25
Driver (delivery)	5.00

Source: Adapted from *Survey of Wages for Hourly Employees,* National Restaurant Association, Washington, D.C., 1990.

and performance. Benefits such as tuition reimbursement and employee recognition programs emphasize growth and achievement and will typically be used by high achievers. Other benefits such as health and life insurance meet employees' health and security needs and, because they are given equally to high and low achievers, have no motivational value. They are simply a cost of doing business.

To attract and retain employees, a competitive benefits package is necessary. It is therefore important for you to find out what other comparable businesses in your area are offering. A benefits survey can be done at the same time you do your wage surveys.

There is no single benefits program that satisfies everyone's needs. Different groups of employees have separate needs. The time has passed when an employer could design a benefits program with a married man with two to three children in mind. Consider your employees' age, sex, marital status, number of dependents, and length of service. Better yet, allow for employee input through committees, surveys, or another method. Review periodically the benefits program to be sure that it is meeting the needs of employees.

When developing a program, you must also consider the amount of money available, the cost of the program's administration, and various laws affecting benefits programs. Be sure to get professional advice from your insurance, legal, and accounting advisers.

There are many options available for inclusion in a benefits program. A listing of possible employee benefits follows:

LEGALLY REQUIRED BENEFITS

Social Security
Workers' compensation
Unemployment insurance

HEALTH AND LIFE INSURANCE

Health insurance
- Group health
- Health Maintenance Organizations

Dental insurance
Vision care
Hearing
Drugs/prescriptions
Life insurance
- Group life

Disability/accident insurance
- Accidental death and disability
- Long-term disability
- Short-term disability

PENSIONS/CAPITAL ACCUMULATION PLANS

Pension plan
Employee stock ownership plan
401(k) plan
Profit sharing

PAYMENT FOR TIME NOT WORKED

Breaks
Sick leave
Vacation time
Personal time banks (Time accrued is used for sick days and vacation days.)
Holidays

Personal
Bereavement
Bonus days off (for good attendance, etc.)
Jury duty
Excused voting time

PAID OR UNPAID TIME OFF

Maternity leave
Paternity leave
Family leave
Extended leave
Other personal leaves

EMPLOYEE SERVICES AND OTHER BENEFITS

Flexible hours
Awards, such as for length of service and incentives
Performance recognition
Bonuses
Educational assistance
Meals/meal allowances
Uniforms/uniform allowances
Parking/parking cost assistance
Employee savings plans, loans, credit unions, and thrift plans
Direct deposit of payroll checks
Stock ownership purchase plans
Employee assistance program
Health and fitness services
Social and recreational programs
Payroll deduction for additional insurance
Legal services
Discounts to employee family members
Discount purchases
Financial planning services
Preretirement planning and counseling
Relocation (moving) expenses
Child-care availability/child-care assistance
Holiday (or other) gifts
Membership in professional and trade associations
Attendance at industry seminars
Trade journals and periodicals
Scholarships for dependent children
Matched employee donations (universities and colleges)

HEALTH INSURANCE

In 1983, the most expensive benefit paid by employers was retirement/Social Security. In 1988, health insurance became the most expensive benefit.

Employees prefer health insurance over most other benefits, and the wide majority of employers in the United States do offer health insurance to their employees. The National Restaurant Association's Survey of Health Insurance Coverage in the Restaurant Industry (1987) found that small companies are less likely to provide health insurance coverage. As sales volume increases, so does the possibility of providing coverage for salaried and hourly personnel. For instance, 33 percent of hourly employees were covered by health insurance in restaurants with under $500,000 sales volume. This figure increases to 59 percent in restaurants with a sales volume between $500,000 and $999,999.

The most common features of health plans include 90-day waiting periods, maximum coverage of $1 million, coverage of dependents, 30 to 40 hours of work per week required to qualify, and payment by the plan of 80 percent of the costs after the employee pays the deductible amount.

The survey also found that employers are paying 50 percent more toward health insurance than in 1985. An increasing number of employers are asking their employees to contribute to payment of premiums. There is also a growing trend for employers to offer employees the option of joining a Health Maintenance Organization (HMO). An HMO is a medical organization of physicians and other health-care professionals who provide outpatient and hospital services to employees who enroll voluntarily under a prepaid plan. Some HMOs require a minimal copayment (for example, $2) for each use of the service. Plan members must use HMO-approved physicians and hospitals. HMOs emphasize preventive care to provide early treatment and to keep costs down.

As a general rule, the larger the employer, the greater the number of supplemental health benefits available to employees. The most popular benefits include dental plans, followed by prescription drug plans and vision care plans.

LIFE INSURANCE AND DISABILITY/ACCIDENT INSURANCE

Group life insurance is also a widely available employee benefit, although employee preference for it is not high. Workers' compensation is designed to cover only short-term disability; therefore long-term disability insurance is often needed. The most popular plans to cover disabilities and accidents are accidental death and disability (AD&D) and long-term disability (LTD) insurance. The majority of long-term disability and accident disability insurance plans pay benefits for up to 26 weeks.

PENSIONS

Many employers offer some type of retirement or pension plan. Some plans are noncontributory, which means that the employee does not contribute; the employer bears the entire cost. Most pension plans are categorized as either defined benefit pension plans or defined contribution plans. In defined benefit pension plans, the amount of the pension upon retirement and the conditions for its payment are known ahead of time. In defined contribution plans, there is a preset determination as to how the employer, and possibly the employee, will contribute to the pension fund, which may be through profit sharing, Independent Retirement Accounts (IRAs), and so forth. However, the amount of the actual pension will not be determined until retirement, when the value of the funds will be determined.

Among defined contribution plans, salary reduction or 401(k) plans, named after Section 401(k) of the Internal Revenue Code, are the most popular. Employees, particularly in small businesses, can save for retirement through payroll deductions, which are not taxed, and possibly have their savings matched by their employer. In most 401(k) plans, full vesting occurs immediately or within 5 years. Full vesting means that the person has a right to the pension should he or she leave the company. The 1986 Tax Reform Act limits the salary deferral to $7,000, which will rise slightly as the cost of living increases.

EMPLOYEE SERVICES AND OTHER BENEFITS

Many of the employee services and other benefits listed here are discussed in various parts of this book. This section will address child-care availability and assistance, and educational assistance.

The percentage of working mothers with children under 6 years of age increased from 47 percent in the mid-1980s to 56 percent in 1988. In addition to the growing number of mothers in the work force, the number of women of childbearing age is projected to increase 12 percent from 1988 to the year 2000. The issue of child care is particularly important for foodservice operators, because in 1988 females made up about 60 percent of hourly employees and 40 percent of salaried employees. Of even greater importance is that 40 percent of employees in foodservice are females in their childbearing years, ages 18 to 44.

In a 1989 nationwide survey by the Gallup Organization and the Employee Benefit Research Institute, 71 percent of respondents said that employers should do something to provide adequate child care. Child-care assistance helps to meet the needs of mothers in the work force to have affordable child care while they work. Such assistance may be accomplished in many different ways.

1. Providing direct or support services
   - On-site child care
   - Off-site child care
   - Care for sick child
2. Providing information
   - Referral services
   - Information on parent education
3. Providing financial assistance
   - Discounts
   - Vouchers
   - Flexible spending accounts
   - Flexible benefits
4. Easing time constraints
   - Flexible hours
   - Part-time work
   - Personal leave

Although employees most often prefer on-site or near-site day care, this option presents difficulties. Two concerns with running a facility of this type are legal liability and cost.

On the other hand, providing flexible spending accounts helps the employee and actually costs the employer little or nothing. Such an account allows the employee to designate a certain percentage of her salary for the employer to apply to child care. The employee is exempt from paying taxes on that portion of earnings, and the employer is exempt from Social Security payments on it as well. The cost of establishing and administering the account is more than offset by the Social Security tax savings.

A 1987 Bureau of Labor Statistics study of 10,000 businesses and government agencies that had at least 10 employees revealed that approximately 11 percent provided some employees with child-care assistance. In a 1989 National Restaurant Associaton survey, it was shown that less than 2 percent of those surveyed subsidized any child-care expenses for salaried or hourly employees. When employees did receive child-care assistance, they were eligible to receive it immediately and in most cases were not required to work a minimum number of hours to receive it. Almost all employers reported providing flexible work schedules and time off to care for a sick child.

Although foodservice operators have not been as quick as other businesses to embrace the idea of child-care assistance, some operators are trying it out. For example, Marriott is working on offering on-site child care at its health-care, business and industry, and education accounts, by joining Corporate Child Care Inc., a provider of employer-sponsored day care, in a joint venture.

For many employees between 18 and 24 years old, tuition reimbursement can be a valuable incentive since many of them want to obtain an education. Examples of successful programs include the following:

Au Bon Pain, a fast-food chain, offers to employees who have worked at least 750 hours either a $1,000 scholarship or a $500 bonus.

Chick-Fil-A, another fast-food chain, offers scholarships to crew members who have worked for at least 2 years.

Burger King allows employees to build up to $2,000 worth of tuition credits in 2 years, starting after an employee has been on board for 3 months. The program is financed by each unit and operated like the GI Bill.

Another method was used by an owner and operator of two Burger Kings in Detroit who worked with local community colleges to begin an educational incentive program. Based on the number of hours worked per week, the cost of tuition and books was paid for one, two, or three courses. The more hours worked, the more courses were paid for. There was no prerequisite work experience required, and the employee was only obliged to meet with a counselor at the college for advice when registering for courses. In an 8-month study, results showed a 39 percent turnover rate for employees using the program, as compared with a 160 percent turnover for employees who did not take advantage of the program. The turnover rate for high school students was 118 percent.

FLEXIBLE BENEFIT PROGRAMS

Flexible benefit programs, also called flex, cafeteria, or employee choice plans, offer participants options in terms of which benefits they want and the types of coverage. Employers implement flexible plans in order to control the spiraling costs of benefits, better meet the different needs of employees, improve employee satisfaction and morale, and educate employees about actual benefit costs. Flexible benefit programs have been in existence since the early 1970s, and although they are not widely used at present, their numbers are growing.

In a flexible benefit program, employees are given a menu of benefit choices and told how much money the employer has allotted for the program, as well as which aspects of the program are mandatory. The three most common flexible benefits are health insurance, life insurance, and dental care.

Flexible benefit plans also often have a feature called a reimbursement account or a flexible spending account. An employee can set aside pretax dollars to pay for goods or services not covered by the benefit plan. These might include contact lenses or dental work not covered by the dental plan.

Flexible benefit programs are not practical for every organization. To start them is costly and time-consuming. Because the idea is new and somewhat strange to employees, much time and money are needed to communicate the program to them and help them make benefit choices.

In summary, for benefits to help in retaining your employees, it is important to do the following:

Involve your employees in initiating or revising your benefits program. You can achieve participation by doing surveys or setting up an employee benefits advisory committee.

Make sure your benefits program meets the needs of your employees better than that of your competitors.

Communicate to your employees the benefits to which they are entitled. Use newsletters, booklets, bulletin boards, letters mailed to employees' homes, payroll stuffers, or meetings.

38. Provide a Reasonable Work Schedule

To the extent possible, try to meet the scheduling needs of your employees. Keep in mind that today's employees have many important obligations outside their jobs, such as college courses or care of children, a home, and/or aging parents. If you want them to stay at their jobs, you must try to accommodate some of their needs. One very popular way to do this is to institute flexible scheduling.

Avoid asking your employees to work too many hours and become very stressed. You show little regard for employees when you make unreasonable demands on their time. It is difficult for anyone to have a satisfactory personal life when working nights, weekends, and holidays, in addition to regular hours.

39. Provide a Pleasant, Safe, and Clean Work Environment

Employees like to work, as we all do, in a pleasant, safe, and clean environment. Can you answer yes to all of the following questions?

Do your employees have enough room in which to do their jobs?
Do the work areas have enough lighting?
Is your kitchen air-conditioned?
Does your kitchen have sufficient air circulation to remove odors, grease, and humidity?
Is the physical environment cheerful and bright?
Is your operation kept clean?
Are safety concerns addressed quickly?
Are employees trained properly in how to use hazardous chemicals?
Are your employees familiar with basic sanitation and safety rules?
Do your employees apply basic sanitation and safety rules?
Do your employees know what to do in case of fire or injury?
Do you have a first aid kit available, and do employees know where it is and how to use it?
Do your employees have adequate equipment and tools to do their jobs?
Do you provide adequate and safe parking for your employees?

Appendixes D and E contain detailed foodservice sanitation and safety checklists. They can be used on a regular basis, such as once a month, to maintain a safe and clean kitchen.

Although it is unlikely that a person will quit his or her job only because of poor working conditions (such as a poorly lit kitchen), it is likely that an applicant who observes an uninviting environment will not want to come to work for you. In addition, a continual problem that is not corrected may become an irritant which, when coupled with other drawbacks such as uninteresting work, may make another employer appear very attractive.

40. Have Fun While You Work

Make your workplace fun. Humor is any communication that elicits laughter, smiles, or a feeling of amusement. It may take the form of teasing, joking, witticisms, puns, clowning, joke telling, or practical jokes.

Humor serves many valuable purposes. It helps to break the ice, encourages a sense of trust, and establishes feelings of camaraderie and friendship. Laughter brings people closer together and therefore can form a bond between members of work teams. Humor can also effect a more relaxed atmosphere by relieving anxiety, anger, and tension.

Tips on How to Make Your Workplace Fun

- Smile a lot.
- Laugh a lot. Laughter is contagious!
- Encourage employees to smile, have a sense of humor, and laugh a lot.
- Poke fun at yourself by laughing at what you do, not at who you are. It lets your employees know that you are human and that you can take things seriously enough to joke about them. By being able to laugh at some of the mistakes you make, you encourage your employees to admit and learn from theirs. Work at taking your job seriously and yourself lightly.
- Avoid sarcastic humor, ethnic humor, and laughing at, instead of with, others.
- Make your memos humorous by using humorous statements or anecdotes. See Fig. 7-2.
- Use humor to handle the uneasiness of change and to build teamwork.
- During a stressful moment, try one of the following one-liners to reduce everyone's stress level.

"Are we having fun yet?"
"This too shall pass."
"The only light at the end of the tunnel is the train coming right this way."
"I've only got one nerve left. How did you ever find it?"

In summary, the cheapest benefit you can offer your employees is laughter. When you try to make your workplace fun, your employees want to come to work.

Fig. 7-2 A HUMOROUS MEMO

MEMORANDUM

To: ALL EMPLOYEES
From: Jane Smith, General Manager
Date: September 1, 1991
Subject: Performance Evaluations

Effective immediately all employees will be evaluated using this rating guide. Please review carefully.

Performance Rating Guide

Performance Factors	Far Exceeds Job Requirements	Exceeds Job Requirements	Meets Job Requirements	Needs Some Improvement	Does Not Meet Minimum Requirements
Quality	Leaps Tall Buildings with a Single Bound	Must Take Running Start to Leap Over Tall Buildings	Can Leap Over Short Buildings Only	Crashes Into Buildings When Attempting to Jump Over Them	Cannot Recognize Buildings at All
Timeliness	Is Faster than a Speeding Bullet	Is as Fast as a Speeding Bullet	Not Quite as Fast as a Speeding Bullet	Would You Believe a Slow Bullet?	Wounds Self with Bullet When Attempting to Shoot
Initiative	Is Stronger than a Locomotive	Is Stronger than a Bull Elephant	Is Stronger than a Bull	Shoots the Bull	Smells Like a Bull
Communications	Talks with God	Talks with the Angels	Talks to Himself	Argues with Himself	Loses These Arguments

ASSESSMENT OF CLIMATE-BUILDING SKILLS

Directions: In the blank space at the front of each item, put the number which best indicates your estimation of the frequency of each behavior.

Scale: 5—Never, 4—Seldom, 3—Occasionally, 2—Usually, 1—Always

_____ 38. Provide a reasonable work schedule.
_____ 39. Provide a pleasant, safe, and clean working environment.
_____ 40. Have fun while you work.

The more frequently you use the above behaviors, the better you are at climate-building skills. In any case where you gave yourself a "3" or higher, use the following Checklist to work harder on these skills.

CLIMATE-BUILDING SKILLS CHECKLIST

Directions: Use this checklist at periodic intervals, such as every month, to see how well you are doing in the selected skill areas. Check off the skills you used, as a way to reinforce your positive behaviors, and circle those skills you have not used but wish to. Keep this checklist handy as a reminder of the skills you want to work on.

38. Provide a reasonable work schedule.

DID YOU:

_____ Try to meet the scheduling needs of your employees?
_____ Avoid asking employees to work too many hours?

39. Provide a pleasant, safe, and clean working environment.

DID YOU:

_____ Provide employees with enough room to do their jobs?
_____ Have enough lighting in work areas?
_____ Have sufficient air circulation to remove odors, grease, and humidity?
_____ Keep the temperature at a comfortable level?
_____ Maintain a cheerful and bright physical environment?
_____ Keep everything clean?
_____ Address safety concerns quickly?
_____ Train employees properly on how to use hazardous chemicals?
_____ Train employees on basic sanitation and safety rules?
_____ See employees applying basic sanitation and safety rules?
_____ Have a first aid kit available and make sure employees know where it is and how to use it?
_____ Have adequate equipment and tools for employees to do their jobs?
_____ Have adequate and safe parking for your employees?

CLIMATE-BUILDING SKILLS CHECKLIST Continued

40. Have fun while you work.

DID YOU:

_____ Smile a lot?

_____ Laugh a lot?

_____ Encourage employees to smile, have a sense of humor, and laugh a lot?

_____ Poke fun at yourself by laughing at what you do, not at who you are?

_____ Take your job seriously and yourself lightly?

_____ Avoid sarcastic humor, ethnic humor, and laughing at, instead of with, others?

_____ Make your memos humorous by using humorous statements or anecdotes?

_____ Use humor to handle the uneasiness of change and to build teamwork?

_____ During a stressful moment, try one of the following one-liners to reduce everyone's stress level?

"Are we having fun yet?"

"This too shall pass."

"The only light at the end of the tunnel is the train coming right this way."

"I've only got one nerve left. How did you ever find it?"

Appendix A

Resources for Developing a Wellness Program

National Organizations

American Cancer Society (ACS)
The American Cancer Society's "Taking Control" program provides information on factors that contribute to cancer risks, and suggests healthy life-style changes that may reduce the risk of developing cancer. It is a comprehensive package which enables businesses to address nutrition, weight control, smoking, alcohol, and other cancer-related factors. For companies interested in using the "Taking Control" program, ACS will provide training and speakers as needed, and materials at no cost once the program has been promoted in-house.

For further information on this program or other nutrition services provided by the American Cancer Society, please contact your local ACS chapter.

The American Dietetic Association (ADA)
The American Dietetic Association is the nation's largest professional organization for more than 52,000 dietitians, dietetic technicians, and nutritionists, with affiliates in all 50 states. Members have expertise in all areas of dietetic and nutrition practice, including counseling, nutrition education, health promotion and foodservice management. ADA has several special interest practice groups that have a worksite focus. These include Sports and Cardiovascular Nutritionists, Dietitians in Business and Industry, and Consulting Nutritionists in Private Practice.

ADA and its Foundation are establishing a National Center for Nutrition and Dietetics which will serve as a clearinghouse for materials, resources, and references. The Center will conduct training seminars and provides materials for employers and health professionals in areas such as diet and heart disease, hypertension, fitness, and obesity. The Association also has consumer education materials in these same areas, and sponsors National Nutrition Month each March.

For further information about ADA's services, contact a local or state chapter, or the national headquarters: Division of Practice, The American Dietetic Association, 216 West Jackson Boulevard, Chicago, IL 60606-6995.

American Heart Association (AHA)
The American Heart Association is a nonprofit, voluntary health organization dedicated to the reduction of premature death and disability from cardiovascular disease and stroke. The Association works toward this goal through programs in research, professional education, and public education. Brochures, audiovisuals, directories, position papers, guidelines, and fact sheets are available on diet and nutrition. The National Center of AHA has developed "Heart at Work," a comprehensive health promotion program specifically tailored for use by businesses. Nutrition is one of the five components included in this program. Any or all of the components can be used alone or integrated into existing worksite health promotion activities.

For further information about these and other AHA programs and services, contact your local AHA office.

American Red Cross
The American Red Cross is a private, nonprofit organization that offers health education programs in a variety of areas, including nutrition, hypertension control, first aid, and cardiopulmonary resuscitation (CPR). The Red Cross nutrition course, "Better Eating for Better Health," provides participants with a set of nutrition "survival skills" to help them apply current nutrition knowledge to their own life-styles. This course is implemented by local chapters and can be offered through existing worksite health promotion programs. The course is taught for a fee by trained, certified Red Cross instructors.

For further information concerning the course, contact your local Red Cross chapter.

March of Dimes
The March of Dimes Birth Defects Foundation is a nonprofit, voluntary health organization dedicated to preventing birth defects and improving the outcome of pregnancy. Their "Good Health is Good Business" program is a preventive health education program for the workplace offered by local March of Dimes chapters at no cost. The

program includes free educational seminars and a variety of audiovisual and print materials. The primary target audience is women in the child-bearing years (16 to 44 years old), but a variety of employees will find the health message pertinent.

Topics for the "Good Health is Good Business" program are genetics; prenatal care; nutrition and exercise; smoking, alcohol, and drugs; environmental influences; teenage pregnancy; seminars for parents; and stress and pregnancy. The program is taught by volunteer health professionals working with local chapters. The program is flexible so the employer can choose which topics will be presented and the desired length of program sessions.

To find out more about this program, contact your local March of Dimes chapter, or write to the national office: Director, Business Health Programs, March of Dimes, 1275 Mamaroneck Avenue, White Plains, NY 10605.

National Dairy Council (NDC)

The National Dairy Council is a nonprofit education and scientific organization which focuses on nutrition research and nutrition education. There are 33 affiliated Dairy Council units with 127 offices across the country. NDC recently initiated the "Lifesteps: Weight Management" program to provide worksites with trained staff and materials to conduct a 13-week weight management course.

For further information, contact your local Dairy Council affiliate, or the National Dairy Council, 6300 N. River Road, Rosemont, IL 60018.

Society for Nutrition Education (SNE)

The Society for Nutrition Education, a nonprofit professional organization, communicates nutrition education research, concepts, and issues to employers, health professionals, and consumers for the purpose of improving the health of the public. In the spring of 1986, SNE published a special supplement to the *Journal of Nutrition Education* on "Nutrition at the Worksite." This special journal includes articles about worksite nutrition programs, reviews and listings of educational materials, and a directory of providers and programs. SNE provides films, bibliographies, and publications on health and nutrition; conducts training on worksite nutrition topics; and operates a Resource Lending Service for print and audiovisual materials (SNE Resource Lending Service, 321 Wallace Avenue, Vallejo, CA 94590).

For further information about available materials and services, contact: Society for Nutrition Education, 1736 Franklin Street, Suite 900, Oakland, CA 94612.

Government Agencies

U.S. DEPARTMENT OF AGRICULTURE

Cooperative Extension Service. The Cooperative Extension Service has 3,000 county offices throughout the United States. The Extension Service conducts informal education programs, and is a good source for low-cost print materials about nutrition education, the Dietary Guidelines, food preparation, and food safety. Extension home economists can conduct brown bag seminars on a variety of topics, and may also be able to help worksites design nutrition programs. Local agents also can refer callers to other sources of information.

Contact your county extension office or state land grant university for information about the Cooperative Extension agents in your area.

Food and Nutrition Information Center. The Food and Nutrition Information Center (FNIC) acquires books, journal articles, and audiovisual materials about human nutrition, nutrition education, foodservice management, and food technology. Worksite health promotion managers can obtain a variety of print and audiovisual materials for their programs at minimal cost through FNIC's lending and reference service.

For further information or a catalog of materials, contact: U.S. Department of Agriculture, Food and Nutrition Information Center, National Agricultural Library, Room 304, Beltsville, MD 20705.

U.S. DEPARTMENT OF HEALTH AND HUMAN SERVICES (DHHS)

National Cancer Institute. The National Cancer Institute (NCI) conducts research and disseminates information on the diagnosis, treatment, and prevention of cancer. NCI has produced excellent pamphlets on cancer prevention, which can be used in business settings. Two such publications are "Good News: Better News: Best News" and "Diet, Nutrition, and Cancer Prevention: A Guide to Food Choices."

For further information, contact: Office of Cancer Communications, National Cancer Institute, Building 31, Room 10A-18, 9000 Rockville Pike, Bethesda, MD 20205.

ODPHP Health Information Center. The ODPHP Health Information Center (OHIC) (formerly the National Health Information Clearinghouse) is operated as a free service to the public by the Office of Disease Prevention and Health Promotion (ODPHP). It is a centralized source of information and provides referral for a broad range of health and nutrition questions, including those concerning worksite health promotion. The Center carries worksite-specific resource materials and a bibliography to aid in health promotion program development, as well as the *Dietary Guidelines for Americans.*

Contact: OHIC, 1255 23rd Street, N.W., Suite 275, Washington, DC 20037.

National Heart, Lung, and Blood Institute. The National Heart, Lung, and Blood Institute (NHLBI) conducts and supports research and education on diseases of the heart, lung, and blood. NHLBI is active in two categorical programs with nutrition and worksite components: the National Cholesterol Education Program and the National High Blood Pressure Education Program. The NHLBI Workplace Initiative supports research and education for reduction of cardiovascular risk factors. Nutrition efforts figure prominently in this initiative.

For further information, contact: Coordinator for Workplace Activities, Office of Prevention, Education, and Control, National Heart, Lung, and Blood Institute, Building 31, Room 4A18, Bethesda, MD 20892.

Appendix B

Training Class Outlines*

This appendix provides outlines for training classes on safe food handling and using recipes. Each class outline starts with these four headings.

1. *Learning Objectives.* The learning objectives are designed to answer the question, "What do I want my employees to get out of this training?"
2. *Handouts.* The handout materials, such as exercises or quizzes, are listed here and appear after "Other Teaching Ideas."
3. *Time Required.* This is only a general guideline, because time will vary depending on the size of the class, how successful the trainer is at getting the employees talking, and so forth.
4. *Evaluation.* The evaluation techniques listed are meant to answer the question, "Did the employees learn the new information, use the new skills, and demonstrate new attitudes after the training?"

The remainder of the class outline is broken down into these sections: Introduction, Learning Objectives, Summary, Other Teaching Ideas, and Handouts. Because these are the actual outlines you will use in class, they have two columns. The left column, Key Concepts, contains the content of the class—in other words, what to teach. The right column, Trainer's Directions, gives instructions on how to teach it.

* Adapted from *The Health Care Food Service Training Manual* by K. Drummond with permission of Aspen Publishers, Inc., © 1990.

1. *Introduction.* The purpose of this section is to interest employees in the topic and to introduce the learning objectives so that employees know what the class will be about and how it will benefit them. You will notice on the class outlines that there is an Introduction A and an Introduction B. Choose whichever one you think employees will enjoy more. You will also notice that the names of teaching methods, such as Guided Discussion, are listed after the Introduction headings. Descriptions of most methods appear on pages 47–49.
2. *Learning Objectives.* The class outline is broken down by learning objectives. Again, teaching methods are listed below the objectives. Additional teaching ideas for learning objectives are found at the end of the class outline.
3. *Summary.* At the end of each class are a Summary A and a Summary B. Again, choose whichever one you feel will work best to meet your and your employees' needs.

You may wish to use videotapes as part of these classes. They are an excellent means of training when you also provide a warm-up, discussion of main points, summary, and evaluation.

4

Safe Food-Handling Techniques*

LEARNING OBJECTIVES

The employee will be able to

1. recognize major factors leading to foodborne illness
2. apply safe food-handling techniques

HANDOUTS

1. Warm-Up Questions
2. Exercise
3. Quiz A
4. Quiz B
5. Safe Food-Handling/Techniques

TIME REQUIRED 20–30 minutes

EVALUATION

1. Written quiz
2. Coaching

Key Concepts	Trainer's Directions

INTRODUCTION

Introduction A

Warm-up Questions

1. An outbreak of food poisoning can cause which of the following problems?
   a. loss of customers and sales
   b. loss of reputation

Introduction A: Exercise

- Pass out Handout #1, Warm-Up Questions, and ask the employees to complete it in five minutes.
- Review the correct answers.

*The correct answers are shown in italics.

Key Concepts	Trainer's Directions

c. low employee morale
d. need to retrain employees
e. *all of the above*

2. An average cost to a food service for an outbreak of food poisoning (to cover medical and legal fees, etc.) is
   a. $10,000
   b. $50,000
   c. *$75,000*
3. The amount of time it takes 8 gallons of soup to cool down to 60° from 140°F in a stockpot is
   a. one hour
   b. two hours
   c. three hours
   d. *four hours*
4. Leftover foods should be
   a. covered
   b. labeled with the name
   c. labeled with the date
   d. *all of the above*
5. The #1 factor that contributes to foodborne illness is
   a. *inadequate cooling*
   b. inadequate cooking
   c. infected employees
   d. a day or more between cooking and serving

- Explain the learning objectives

Introduction B

The number of hours needed to cool 8 gallons of soup from 140° to 60°F in a stockpot is 4 hours.

Introduction B: Game

- Ask the employees to guess the number of hours it takes 8 gallons of soup to cool down from 140° to 60°F in a stockpot. Give a prize to the employee who comes closest to the correct answer.
- Explain the learning objectives.

Key Concepts	Trainer's Directions

LEARNING OBJECTIVES

Learning Objective 1

The employee will be able to recognize major factors leading to foodborne illness.

The five major factors leading to foodborne illness are
1. inadequate cooling
2. a day or more between cooking and serving
3. infected employees
4. inadequate cooking
5. inadequate hot storage

Exercise
- Pass out Handout #2, Exercise. Ask employees to complete it by ranking the five major factors or reasons for foodborne illness. Review the correct ranking, which is given in the left column.

Learning Objective 2

The employee will be able to apply safe food-handling techniques.

Following are the ten necessities of safe food handling.
1. Keep foods out of the Danger Zone (45°–140°F).
   - Handle foods quickly during delivery, and put refrigerated and frozen foods away as soon as possible.
   - Thaw foods in the refrigerator or under cold running water for not more than 2 hours.
   - Handle foods quickly during preparation.
   - Cook and serve foods at a temperature of over 140°F.

Guided discussion/demonstration
- Discuss the ten necessities of safe food handling. Ask the employees to give you ideas on how to apply each one, and write them on a board or easel pad. Be sure to cover all the key concepts. Demonstrate and ask "Why?" as directed.
- Emphasize that foods should never be thawed at room temperature.

Key Concepts	Trainer's Directions
Heat leftovers to at least 165°F.	
• To cool down hot foods, use shallow pans and/or an ice bath. Stir hot foods to remove heat. Cut large pieces of meat, etc., into smaller pieces to allow heat loss.	• Show the class examples of shallow pans (2½ inches deep). You may want to demonstrate an ice bath: pans of food are placed in ice water.
• Use thermometers to check food temperature during storing, cooking, serving, cooling, and reheating. Put the thermometer into the center or the thickest part of the food at least up to the dimple on the stem.	• Demonstrate how to use a thermometer by putting it into the center or thickest part of the food. Show that the thermometer must be immersed up to the dimple on the stem in order to get an accurate reading.
2. Inspect foods thoroughly for freshness and wholesomeness upon receipt and before cooking and serving.	
• Check incoming canned goods for rusted, dented, and bulging cans.	• Ask "Why?" Dented and rusted cans may indicate the growth of a bacteria in the can that causes a deadly disease, botulism.
• Check other incoming goods for proper temperature and freshness.	
• Be sure to use the foods that have been in storage the longest first.	
• Check that foods are not outdated.	
• Check for off colors and odors.	
• Do not use eggs that are cracked.	• Ask "Why?" They may contain significant amounts of a bacteria that will cause foodborne illness.
• Wash thoroughly raw foods such as fruits and vegetables before use.	
• When in doubt, throw it out.	

Key Concepts	Trainer's Directions
3. Store foods properly.	
• Cover, label, and date foods in storage.	• Explain your policy.
• Store supplies off the floor and away from the wall.	• Ask "Why?" It helps prevent pests and animals from getting a free meal.
• Rotate foods.	
• Check the temperatures of refrigerators and freezers daily.	
• Defrost freezers as necessary. Frost buildup causes freezers to warm up.	
• Storage areas for dry goods should be cool and dry to maintain good food quality.	
• Do not store food under exposed sewer or water lines.	
• Keep storage areas clean.	
• Do not store food in open cans.	
• Store chemicals and pesticides separately from food.	• Ask "Why?" This helps prevent contamination of the food.
4. Clean and sanitize all equipment, tools, tables, dishes, etc., after each use.	• This topic is discussed in detail in Class 5.
• Store wiping cloths in sanitizing solution.	
• Store equipment, tools, etc., so they do not collect dust.	
5. Avoid letting the microorganisms from one food contaminate another food.	
• Use separate cutting boards for raw and cooked foods.	
• Clean utensils and knives after each use.	
• Never mix leftovers with fresh food.	

Key Concepts	Trainer's Directions
• Store fresh raw meats, poultry, and fish on the lowest shelves.	• Ask "Why?" In this manner, if these foods drip, they will not contaminate other foods.
• Sanitize thermometers after each use.	• Demonstrate this by using an alcohol swab or a sanitizing solution. Explain your policy.
6. Observe good grooming and hygiene practices.	• This is covered in detail in Class 2.
• Keep healthy.	
• Practice good grooming.	
• Practice good on-the-job personal hygiene.	
7. Avoid preparing food further in advance than absolutely necessary.	
8. Dispose of waste properly.	
• Cover garbage cans.	
• Remove garbage regularly.	• Review your policy.
• Clean and sanitize garbage cans.	• Review your policy.
• Throw out food that was served but not eaten (unless it is wrapped), falls on the floor, is outdated, does not meet quality standards, was exposed to hazardous chemicals, was in the Danger Zone for over 3 hours, or was otherwise mishandled.	
• Store soiled linen in a laundry bag or nonabsorbent container.	
	• You may also want to note for safety reasons that dangerous objects such as broken glass, broken dishes, and can lids should be disposed of in a separate receptacle labeled for that purpose.

Key Concepts	**Trainer's Directions**
9. Keep insects and animals out. • Keep doors closed. • Take garbage out frequently. • Keep garbage areas clean and garbage sealed. • Report any holes where an animal could enter. • Do not provide a free meal. • Keep work areas clean and uncluttered.	
10. Handle ice properly.	
• Use clean scoops or tongs to pick up ice. Do not use your hands or a glass.	• Ask "Why?" Hands carry bacteria, and a glass might chip in the ice.
• Store scoops or tongs in a clean container, not in the ice.	• Ask "Why?" This minimizes contamination.
• Do not store any food or beverage in the ice.	• Ask "Why?" This prevents contamination of the ice.

SUMMARY

Summary A	Summary A: Summary
Following are the ten necessities of safe food handling. 1. Keep foods out of the Danger Zone (45°–140°F). 2. Inspect foods thoroughly for freshness and wholesomeness upon receipt and before cooking and serving. 3. Store food properly. 4. Clean and sanitize all equipment, tools, tables, dishes, etc., after each use. 5. Avoid letting the microorganisms from one food contaminate another food.	• Review the ten necessities of safe food handling.

Key Concepts	Trainer's Directions
6. Observe good grooming and hygiene practices. 7. Avoid preparing food further in advance than absolutely necessary. 8. Dispose of waste properly. 9. Keep insects and animals out. 10. Handle ice properly.	
	• Ask the employees to complete Handout #3 or #4, Quiz A or B, and hand it in. • Pass out Handout #5, Safe Food-Handling Techniques, as the employees leave.
Summary B	Summary B: Exercise
	• Do or redo the Warm-Up Questions (see Introduction A). You may want to read each question out loud and ask for the correct answer. • Ask the employees to complete Handout #3 or #4, Quiz A or B, and hand it in. • Pass out Handout #5, Safe Food-Handling Techniques, as the employees leave.

OTHER TEACHING IDEAS

1. For learning Objective 2, you can use buzz groups. Ask the employees to work in small groups (two to four people), utes, ask one member from each group to read his or her list to you as you write the usable ideas on a board or easel pad. To make this into a game, you may offer prizes to the group with the largest number of usable answers for each category or overall. Be sure all possible. After 10 to 15 min- and have each group list as many applications of each necessity of safe food handling as the Key Concepts are covered.
2. Ask a sanitation inspector to teach or assist in teaching one or more of the learning objectives. Ask this person to give actual examples of poor food handling that led to a foodborne outbreak.

Safe Food-Handling Techniques
Handout #1

Warm-Up Questions

Directions: Circle the correct answer.

1. An outbreak of food poisoning can cause which of the following problems?
   a. loss of customers and sales
   b. loss of reputation
   c. low employee morale
   d. need to retrain employees
   e. all of the above

2. An average cost to a food service for an outbreak of food poisoning (to cover medical and legal fees, etc.) is
   a. $10,000
   b. $50,000
   c. $75,000

3. The amount of time it takes 8 gallons of soup to cool down to 60° from 140°F in a stockpot is
   a. one hour
   b. two hours
   c. three hours
   d. four hours

4. Leftover food should be
   a. covered
   b. labeled with the name
   c. labeled with the date
   d. all of the above

5. The #1 factor that contributes to foodborne illness is
   a. inadequate cooling
   b. inadequate cooking
   c. infected employees
   d. a day or more between cooking and serving

Safe Food-Handling Techniques Handout #2

Exercise

Directions: Following are the five major factors that cause foodborne illness. Rank them in order of greatest to least importance, using the numbers 1 to 5.

Factor	Ranking
Infected employees	______________
Inadequate hot storage	______________
Inadequate cooling	______________
A day or more between cooking and serving	______________
Inadequate cooking	______________

Name: ______________________________

Date: ______________________________

Safe Food-Handling Techniques Handout #3

Quiz A

Directions: Circle either True or False.

1. Meats should be thawed at room temperature because it is the fastest method.
   True
   False

2. Soups, stews, and sauces should be cooled in shallow pans and stirred to help release the heat.
   True
   False

3. Leftovers should be heated to at least 150°F.
   True
   False

4. Cooked leftovers should be chilled to a temperature under 45°F in less than 4 hours.
   True
   False

5. Wiping cloths should be stored in a sanitizing solution because they can cause cross-contamination.
   True
   False

6. When you are stocking foods, put the new stock in front of the old stock.
   True
   False

7. It is all right to store raw foods, such as raw meats, on shelves above cooked foods.
   True
   False

8. When storing foods, be sure to label them with the name and date.
   True
   False

9. When in doubt, throw it out.
   True
   False

10. Check the temperature of foods by feel.
    True
    False

Name: ______________________________
Date: ______________________________

Safe Food-Handling Techniques Handout #4

Quiz B

Directions: Below are the ten necessities of safe food handling. For each one, describe a way you will use it in your job.

1. Keep foods out of the Danger Zone (45°–140°F).

2. Inspect foods thoroughly for freshness and wholesomeness upon receipt and before cooking and serving.

3. Store foods properly.

4. Clean and sanitize all equipment, tools, tables, dishes, etc., after each use.

5. Avoid letting microorganisms from one food contaminate another food.

6. Observe good grooming and hygiene practices.

7. Avoid preparing food further in advance than absolutely necessary.

8. Dispose of waste properly.

9. Keep insects and animals out.

10. Handle ice properly.

Name: ______________________________
Date: ______________________________

Safe Food-Handling Techniques Handout #5

Food-Handling Techniques

1. Keep foods out of the Danger Zone (45°–140°F).
2. Inspect foods thoroughly for freshness and wholesomeness upon receipt and before cooking and serving.
3. Store foods properly.
4. Clean and sanitize all equipment, tools, tables, dishes, etc., after each use.
5. Avoid letting the microorganisms from one food contaminate another food.
6. Observe good grooming and hygiene practices.
7. Avoid preparing food further in advance than absolutely necessary.
8. Dispose of waste properly.
9. Keep insects and animals out.
10. Handle ice properly.

24

Using Recipes

LEARNING OBJECTIVES

The employee will be able to

1. cite three limitations of recipes and three ways a good cook can overcome them
2. explain the concept of standardized recipes and two reasons why they are used.
3. correctly convert recipes to higher or lower yields

HANDOUTS

1. Exercise: Recipe Conversion
2. Quiz
3. Using Recipes

TIME REQUIRED 30–45 minutes

EVALUATION

1. Written quiz
2. Coaching

Key Concepts	Trainer's Directions

INTRODUCTION

Introduction A

Introduction A: Guided Discussion

- Ask the employees what recipes they each like to prepare the most. Ask them "Why?" Discuss their responses briefly.
- Explain that today's class is about how to use and convert recipes.
- Explain the learning objectives.

Key Concepts	Trainer's Directions
Introduction B	Introduction B: Lecture • If your operation has a specific format for recipes, review your format at this time. • Explain that today's class is about how to use and convert recipes. • Explain the learning objectives.
LEARNING OBJECTIVES Learning Objective 1 The employee will be able to cite three limitations of recipes and three ways a good cook can overcome them.	
A *recipe* contains both the amount of ingredients and the instructions for a cook to use to make a certain product. A written recipe is vital to producing good dishes, but it cannot tell you everything. Judgment is still needed.	*Lecture/guided discussion* • Explain what a recipe is.
Recipes have the following six limitations. 1. Ingredient quality varies. 2. Equipment and how it is used vary from kitchen to kitchen. 3. The person cooking the food will change. 4. Even the same cook may not prepare a recipe the exact same way every time. 5. The weather and the kitchen's	• Ask the employees for the limitations of recipes and how to overcome them. Write their answers on a board or easel pad. Be sure to cover all the Key Concepts.

Key Concepts	Trainer's Directions
temperature and humidity also vary and will affect how some products turn out. 6. Instructions can never be totally accurate or precise.	
Cooks must use good judgement by • knowing both the characteristics and the purposes of ingredients • knowing how to use basic cooking methods • being familiar with cooking terminology • using cooking times as a guide only and by determining doneness by a product's color, temperature, texture, taste, and/or consistency.	
Learning Objective 2	
The employee will be able to explain the concept of standardized recipes and two reasons why they are used.	
A *standardized recipe* is a written recipe containing a listing of ingredients and the instructions that describe how a particular food service operation makes a menu item. The recipe has been tailored to the operation and takes into account such factors as the equipment available, the quality of the ingredients, and the cooking staff.	*Lecture/guided discussion* • Define *standardized recipe.*

Key Concepts	Trainer's Directions
Standardized recipes are used • to get consistent product quality • to produce consistent quantities • as the basis for cost analysis • as the basis for food purchasing	• Ask the employees for the benefits of using standardized recipes. Write their responses on a board or easel pad. Be sure to cover all the Key Concepts.
Learning Objective 3 The employee will be able to correctly convert recipes to higher or lower yields.	
Follow these two steps to convert a recipe. 1. Divide the desired yield by the current recipe yield to determine the multiplier.	*Tell/show/do/review* • Explain the two steps involved in converting a recipe. • Demonstrate how to do each step.

For example: $\frac{200}{100} = 2$

$$\frac{50}{100} = .5 \text{ or } ½$$

2. Multiply the quantity of each ingredient in the recipe by the multiplier. For example:

Ingredients	*100 servings*	× 2 =	*200 servings*
Flour	12 lb.	× 2=	24 lb.
Water	8 lb.	× 2=	16 lb.
Yeast	6 oz.	× 2=	12 oz.
Shortening	8 oz.	× 2=	16 oz.
Dry milk	1½ lb.	× 2=	3 lb.
Sugar	12 oz.	× 2=	24 oz. = 1½ lb.

Key Concepts	Trainer's Directions
Exercise: Recipe Conversion	• Pass out Handout #1, Exercise: Recipe Conversion, and ask the employees to complete the recipe conversion problems.
1. Your recipe is for 50 portions. You need to adjust it to 125 portions. What is the multiplier? $\frac{125}{50} = 2.5$	• Review the correct answers.
2. Your recipe is for 100 portions. You need to feed only 60. What is the multiplier? $\frac{60}{100} = .6 \text{ or } \frac{6}{10}$	
3. Convert the following recipe to yield 150 portions.	• Explain that it is sometimes easier to convert pounds to ounces and volume measurements to fluid ounces before multiplying. This is the case with the dry milk, which can be converted to 24 oz. × 1.5 = 36 oz. or 2 lb. 4 oz.
Soft Roll Dough	
$\frac{150}{100} = 1.5$	

100 portions	*150 portions*
12 lb. flour	× 1.5 = 18 lb.
8 lb. water	× 1.5 = 12 lb.
6 oz. yeast	× 1.5 = 9 oz.
1½ lb. dry milk	× 1.5 = 2 lb. 4 oz.
12 oz. sugar	× 1.5 = 1 lb. 2 oz.

• If employees use calculators, explain to them that fractions of pounds, such as 0.75, can be converted to ounces by multiplying by 16.

• Explain that some ingredients—such as seasonings, spices, and thickening agents—do not convert well. Converting to a much larger or smaller quantity, such as 8 to 350, can also cause problems.

Key Concepts	Trainer's Directions
SUMMARY	
Summary A	Summary A: Lecture • Review the definition of a recipe and a standardized recipe as well as how a cook is to use good judgment and to convert recipes. • Ask the employees to complete Handout #2, Quiz, and hand it in. • Pass out Handout #3, Using Recipes, as the employees leave.
Summary B	Summary B: Exercise • Using one of your operation's recipes, ask the employees to convert it to a new yield. • Ask the employees to complete Handout #2, Quiz, and hand it in. • Pass out Handout #3, Using Recipes, as the employees leave.
ANOTHER TEACHING IDEA • For Learning Objective 3, have the employees work in pairs on the Exercise.	

Name: ________________________________
Date: ________________________________

Using Recipes
Handout #1

Exercise: Recipe Conversion

1. Your recipe is for 50 portions. You need to adjust it to 125 portions. What is the multiplier?

2. Your recipe is for 100 portions. You need to feed only 60. What is the multiplier?

3. Convert the following recipe to yield 150 portions.

Soft Roll Dough

100 portions	*150 portions*
12 lb. flour	________ flour
8 lb. water	________ water
6 oz. yeast	________ yeast
1½ lb. dry milk	________ dry milk
12 oz. sugar	________ sugar

Name: ______________________________
Date: ______________________________

Using Recipes
Handout #2

Quiz

1. Recipes have limitations such as instructions that can never be totally precise. Describe three ways in which you overcome these limitations.

2. Describe a standardized recipe, and give two reasons why you should use standardized recipes.

3. Your instructor will give you a recipe to convert.

Using Recipes
Handout #3

Using Recipes

A recipe contains both the amount of ingredients and the instructions for a cook to use to make a certain product. A written recipe is vital to producing good dishes, but it cannot tell you everything. Judgment is still needed.

Recipes have the following six limitations.

1. Ingredient quality varies.
2. Equipment and how it is used vary from kitchen to kitchen.
3. The person cooking the food will change.
4. Even the same cook may not prepare a recipe the exact same way every time.
5. The weather and the kitchen's temperature and humidity also vary and will affect how some products turn out.
6. Instructions can never be totally accurate or precise.

These limitations can be overcome in several ways. First, you need to use good judgment by knowing both the characteristics and the purposes of ingredients, as well as by knowing how to use basic cooking methods and being familiar with cooking terminology. Last, you need to use cooking times as a guide only. Determine doneness by a product's color, temperature, texture, taste, and/or consistency.

A standardized recipe is a written recipe containing a listing of ingredients and the instructions that describe how a particular food service operation makes a menu item. The recipe has been tailored to the operation and takes into account such factors as the equipment available, the quality of the ingredients, and the cooking staff.

Standardized recipes are used to get consistent product quality and to produce consistent quantities. They are also used as the basis for cost analysis and food purchasing.

Converting recipes to new yields involves two steps.

1. Divide the desired yield by the current recipe yield to determine the multiplier.
2. Multiply the quantity of each ingredient in the recipe by the multiplier.

Appendix C

Sources for Self-Study Foodservice Courses

American Culinary Federation
P.O. Box 3466
St. Augustine, FL 32084
(904)824-4468

Educational Foundation of the
National Restaurant Association
250 South Wacker Drive
Chicago, IL 60606
(800)522-7578
(312)715-1010

Educational Institute of the
American Hotel and Motel
Association
P.O. Box 1240
East Lansing, MI 48826
(800)752-4567
(517)353-5527

National Restaurant Association
1200 17th Street, N.W.
Washington, DC 20036-3097
(800)424-5156
(202)331-5900

Appendix D

Foodservice Sanitation Checklist

This appendix contains a series of forms that foodservice managers can use to inspect the site for sanitation concerns. Each functional area within the foodservice operation is included in the checklist.

For each area, there are questions which, if answered no, indicate a condition that needs to be corrected.

SANITATION SELF-INSPECTION FORM

AREA: Personal Hygiene INSPECTED BY: DATE:

QUESTION	YES	NO	PROBLEM NOTED	CORRECTIONS	WHEN DONE
1. Do employees avoid touching the food-contact surfaces of plates, cups, and silverware?					
2. Are employees free of boils and other infections (of cuts, burns, and eyes)?					
3. Are employees free of coughs, colds, and other contagious disease?					
4. Are employees wearing clean clothes?					
5. Are employees free of body odors?					
6. Are employees' hands visibly clean?					
7. Are employees' fingernails short and clean?					
8. Are employees wearing hairnets, caps, or other head covering?					
9. Are employees seen smoking or eating only in areas designated for such?					
10. Are employees wearing jewelry in accordance with policy?					

SANITATION SELF-INSPECTION FORM

AREA: Personal Hygiene INSPECTED BY: DATE:

QUESTION	YES	NO	PROBLEM NOTED	CORRECTIONS	WHEN DONE
11. Are employees wearing gloves when appropriate?					
12. Are employees washing their hands properly?					

SANITATION SELF-INSPECTION FORM

AREA: Receiving INSPECTED BY: DATE:

QUESTION	YES	NO	PROBLEM NOTED	CORRECTIONS	WHEN DONE
13. Are supplies inspected for spoilage and infestation during delivery?					
14. Are refrigerated and frozen foods being moved promptly into cold storage?					
15. Are empty boxes and packing materials being disposed of promptly?					
16. Is receiving area, including floor, clean?					
17. Are incoming supplies dated upon receipt to help in using older supplies first?					

SANITATION SELF-INSPECTION FORM

AREA: Dry Stores INSPECTED BY: DATE:

QUESTION	YES	NO	PROBLEM NOTED	CORRECTIONS	WHEN DONE
18. Is all food stored at least 6 inches off the floor and 2 inches away from the wall?					
19. Is the floor clean, especially of spilled foods?					
20. Is all lighting protected by guards, or are bulbs shatterproof?					
21. Are canned goods removed from cartons as much as possible, and cartons disposed of?					
22. Are food storage shelves clean?					
23. Are storage areas cool and dry?					
24. Are nonfood supplies (paper goods and cleaning supplies) stored separately from foods?					
25. Is there *no* evidence of insects or rodents? (Look for droppings and greasy trails running along walls.)					
26. Are bulk foods such as flour, if no longer stored in original packages, now stored in a labeled and covered container?					
27. Are foods *not* stored under exposed or unprotected sewer or water lines?					

SANITATION SELF-INSPECTION FORM

AREA: Refrigerator Storage INSPECTED BY: DATE:

QUESTION	YES	NO	PROBLEM NOTED	CORRECTIONS	WHEN DONE
28. Are refrigerators equipped with accurate thermometers located in the warmest section?					
29. Are all refrigerators maintaining temperatures of 45 degrees or less?					
30. Are floors and walls clean and free from stains?					
31. Are refrigerators free from mold and objectionable odors? (Check rubber moldings for mold.)					
32. Is all food being stored at least 6 inches off the floor and 2 inches from the wall?					
33. Are foods stored on shelves spaced to provide for adequate air circulation?					
34. Are panned raw or cooked foods covered, labeled, and dated?					
35. Are raw foods always on bottom shelves so they do not drip into cooked foods?					
36. Are cooked foods stored in shallow pans and small containers?					
37. Are foods stored in a way to permit first-in, first-out use?					

SANITATION SELF-INSPECTION FORM

AREA: Refrigerator Storage INSPECTED BY: DATE:

QUESTION	YES	NO	PROBLEM NOTED	CORRECTIONS	WHEN DONE
38. Are all foods wholesome and free from visible spoilage?					
39. Are shelves clean?					
40. Is there adequate cold storage capacity to handle normal delivery schedules?					
41. Is all lighting protected by guards, or are bulbs shatterproof?					
42. Is a log of daily refrigerator temperatures available and up-to-date?					

SANITATION SELF-INSPECTION FORM

AREA: Freezer Storage INSPECTED BY: DATE:

QUESTION	YES	NO	PROBLEM NOTED	CORRECTIONS	WHEN DONE
43. Are all freezers equipped with accurate thermometers located in the warmest section?					
44. Are freezers maintaining an interior temperature of 0 degrees or lower?					
45. Is there limited traffic in and out of walk-in freezers?					
46. Is food stored in a way to permit first-in, first-out use?					
47. Is food stored in a manner to allow for air circulation?					
48. Are freezer walls and coils free of ice buildup?					
49. Are foods wrapped well to prevent freezer burn?					
50. Is the floor clean?					
51. Is all food being stored at least 6 inches off the floor and 2 inches from the wall?					
52. Is there enough freezer space to handle normal delivery schedules?					

SANITATION SELF-INSPECTION FORM

AREA: Freezer Storage	INSPECTED BY:			DATE:	
QUESTION	YES	NO	PROBLEM NOTED	CORRECTIONS	WHEN DONE
53. Are all foods labeled, covered, and dated?					
54. Are all lights either shatterproof or covered?					
55. Is a log of daily freezer temperatures available and up-to-date?					

SANITATION SELF-INSPECTION FORM

AREA: Cooking/Food Prep INSPECTED BY: DATE:

QUESTION	YES	NO	PROBLEM NOTED	CORRECTIONS	WHEN DONE
56. Are cooking and food prep floors generally clean?					
57. Is cooking and food prep equipment clean (if not in use)?					
58. Are utensils clean and stored in a way to prevent contamination?					
59. Are cutting boards in good condition, without holes or cuts?					
60. Are cutting boards being cleaned and sanitized between uses?					
61. Are food preparation sinks being used for food preparation only?					
62. Are meats, poultry, and fish being thawed in refrigerator or cold running water?					
63. Is there *no* evidence of rodents or insects in the cooking or food prep areas?					
64. Are bulbs over cooking equipment shatterproof or covered?					
65. Is hot-holding equipment maintaining food at or above 140 degrees?					

SANITATION SELF-INSPECTION FORM

AREA: Cooking/Food Prep INSPECTED BY: DATE:

QUESTION	YES	NO	PROBLEM NOTED	CORRECTIONS	WHEN DONE
66. Are cold foods being held at 45 degrees or lower?					
67. Are employee belongings *not* evident in the cooking/prep areas?					
68. Are cleaning chemicals placed away from food?					
69. Are tables clean, including tops, legs, and underneath?					
70. Is there a convenient handwashing sink with soap and towels available?					
71. Is equipment used for holding and transporting foods clean?					
72. Is equipment used for holding and transporting foods maintaining food under 45 or over 140 degrees?					
73. Are utensils, bowls, etc. stored in a manner to prevent splash and contamination?					

SANITATION SELF-INSPECTION FORM

AREA: Dining Room/Serving Areas   INSPECTED BY: DATE:

QUESTION	YES	NO	PROBLEM NOTED	CORRECTIONS	WHEN DONE
74. Are dining areas, including floor, tables, and chairs, clean?					
75. Is tableware clean and not chipped?					
76. Are single-service items disposed of after single use?					
77. Are tables being cleaned with clean cloths stored in a sanitizing solution?					
78. Are tableware and serving utensils stored in a manner to prevent splash and contamination?					
79. Are foods on counters for customers to pick up protected by sneezeguards?					
80. Are serving area floors clean and free from boxes, etc.?					
81. Is serving equipment clean?					
82. Is beverage equipment clean?					
83. Is there a handwashing sink supplied with soap and paper towels?					

SANITATION SELF-INSPECTION FORM

AREA: Dining Room/Serving Areas INSPECTED BY: DATE:

QUESTION	YES	NO	PROBLEM NOTED	CORRECTIONS	WHEN DONE
84. Are employee belongings *not* evident in these areas?					
85. Are cleaning chemicals placed away from food?					
86. Are all foods being kept below 45 or above 140 degrees?					

SANITATION SELF-INSPECTION FORM

AREA: Ware washing INSPECTED BY: DATE:

QUESTION	YES	NO	PROBLEM NOTED	CORRECTIONS	WHEN DONE
87. Are dishwasher temperatures within specified limits?					
88. Is a log of dishwasher temperatures available and up-to-date?					
89. Is the final rinse temperature at least 170 degrees?					
90. Is tableware scraped and flushed prior to washing?					
91. Are all receptacles for chemicals full on the dishwasher?					
92. Are separate personnel used for removing and storing clean tableware, or do personnel wash their hands between handling soiled and sanitized ware?					
93. Is a handwashing sink available and supplied with soap and paper towels?					
94. Is the dishwasher clean inside and out?					
95. Are jets and nozzles in the dishwasher clear of food particles and other obstructions?					
96. For manual ware washing, are detergent and sanitizer concentrations at proper levels?					

SANITATION SELF-INSPECTION FORM

AREA: Ware washing INSPECTED BY: DATE:

QUESTION	YES	NO	PROBLEM NOTED	CORRECTIONS	WHEN DONE
97. Is a test kit available to check the strength of the sanitizing solution?					
98. Are cleaned and sanitized dishes and utensils stored off the floor and in a clean, dry location free from contamination by splash or dust?					
99. Are dishes, utensils, pots, pans, etc., dry when put away?					
100. Are coffee cups free of stains?					
101. Are floors and walls clean?					

SANITATION SELF-INSPECTION FORM

AREA: Trash Disposal INSPECTED BY: DATE:

QUESTION	YES	NO	PROBLEM NOTED	CORRECTIONS	WHEN DONE
102. Is floor or ground surface clean in trash disposal area?					
103. Is area free from odor?					
104. Are trash containers clean on the outside?					
105. Is trash confined in orderly fashion and in leakproof containers?					
106. Is there *no* evidence of mice or other rodents?					
107. Are empty garbage cans washed prior to being returned for use?					
108. Are hot water, brushes, and detergent or steam provided for washing garbage cans?					
109. Are all garbage cans closed with tight-fitting lids?					

SANITATION SELF-INSPECTION FORM

AREA: Employee Facilities | INSPECTED BY: | DATE:

QUESTION	YES	NO	PROBLEM NOTED	CORRECTIONS	WHEN DONE
110. Are employees' facilities clean and free from odor?					
111. Are there sufficient soap, towels, and tissue?					
112. Are receptacles available for waste materials and are they emptied frequently?					
113. Is there *no* evidence of rodents or insects in the facility?					

Appendix E

Foodservice Safety Checklist

Following is a form that foodservice managers can use to inspect the site for safety concerns. Each functional area within the foodservice operation is included in the checklist.

For each area, there are questions which, if answered no, indicate an unsafe condition to be corrected.

SAFETY SELF-INSPECTION FORM

AREA: Receiving and Dry Storage INSPECTED BY: DATE:

QUESTION	YES	NO	PROBLEM NOTED	CORRECTIONS	WHEN DONE
1. Are floors and walls in safe condition: dry, clean, no tiles missing or broken, no worn areas?					
2. Are ''Wet Floor'' signs available and used when needed?					
3. Is all lighting in working order and adequate?					
4. Are tables, counters, and equipment free from sharp corners and dangerous projections?					
5. Is ventilation sufficient?					
6. Are doors and aisles kept clear of supplies?					
7. Are there sufficient waste receptacles of leakproof, nonabsorbent material?					
8. Are waste receptacles covered?					
9. Is the receiving dock in good repair?					
10. Are incoming supplies being inspected for damage?					

SAFETY SELF-INSPECTION FORM

AREA: Receiving and Dry Storage | INSPECTED BY: | DATE:

QUESTION	YES	NO	PROBLEM NOTED	CORRECTIONS	WHEN DONE
11. Are adequate tools such as wire cutters, cardboard carton openers, and gloves available and being used safely?					
12. Are supplies being lifted properly by employees using leg muscles and not back muscles?					
13. Are hand trucks, carts, and dollies available to transport supplies?					
14. Are hand trucks, carts, and dollies in good repair and not being overloaded?					
15. In storage areas, are dented canned goods set on a special shelf reserved for them?					
16. Are shelves strong enough to hold their loads?					
17. Are storage racks in good condition and standing solidly?					
18. Are heavy items on lower shelves only?					
19. Are the most-used supplies most accessible?					
20. Are supplies stacked neatly and safely?					

SAFETY SELF-INSPECTION FORM

AREA: Receiving and Dry Storage INSPECTED BY: DATE:

QUESTION	YES	NO	PROBLEM NOTED	CORRECTIONS	WHEN DONE
21. Is a ladder available which is solid and in good working condition?					
22. Are supplies stored at least 18 to 24 inches from light bulbs and fire sprinkler heads?					
23. Is there enough storage space so that nothing is stored on the floor or in aisles?					
24. Are hazardous materials kept separate from food?					

SAFETY SELF-INSPECTION FORM

AREA: Refrigerators/ Freezers | INSPECTED BY: | DATE:

QUESTION	YES	NO	PROBLEM NOTED	CORRECTIONS	WHEN DONE
25. Are floors and walls in safe condition: dry, clean, no tiles missing or broken, no worn areas?					
26. Is all lighting in working order and adequate?					
27. Is air circulation sufficient?					
28. Are doors and aisles kept clear of supplies?					
29. Does each walk-in have an alarm bell or a handle to open the door from the inside?					
30. Are shelves strong enough to hold their loads?					
31. Are shelves and equipment free from sharp corners and dangerous projections?					
32. Are storage racks in good condition and standing solidly?					
33. Are heavy items on lower shelves only?					
34. Are the most-used supplies most accessible?					

SAFETY SELF-INSPECTION FORM

AREA: Refrigerators/ Freezers | INSPECTED BY: | DATE:

QUESTION	YES	NO	PROBLEM NOTED	CORRECTIONS	WHEN DONE
35. Are supplies stacked neatly and safely?					
36. Is there enough storage space in each area so that nothing is stored on the floor or in aisles?					
37. Are blower fans clean and guarded?					
38. Are coils clean?					
39. Are freezer coats and gloves available and being used?					

SAFETY SELF-INSPECTION FORM

AREA: Food Preparation Areas INSPECTED BY: DATE:

QUESTION	YES	NO	PROBLEM NOTED	CORRECTIONS	WHEN DONE
40. Are floors and walls in safe condition: dry, clean, no tiles missing or broken, no worn areas?					
41. Are ''Wet Floor'' signs available and used when needed?					
42. Is all lighting in working order and adequate?					
43. Are tables, counters, and equipment free from sharp corners and dangerous projections?					
44. Is ventilation sufficient?					
45. Are doors and aisles kept clear of supplies?					
46. Are there sufficient waste receptacles of leakproof, nonabsorbent material?					
47. Are waste receptacles covered?					
48. Is there enough aisle space to prevent accidents?					
49. Are there enough hot pads and gloves and are they being used?					

SAFETY SELF-INSPECTION FORM

AREA: Food Preparation Areas INSPECTED BY: DATE:

QUESTION	YES	NO	PROBLEM NOTED	CORRECTIONS	WHEN DONE
50. Are lids being lifted carefully to avoid steam burns?					
51. Do employees warn each other when carrying hot food?					
52. Are guards on equipment being used?					
53. Is all equipment working properly?					
54. Are employees using equipment instructed on using it safely?					
55. Is equipment turned off when not in use?					
56. Is electrical equipment grounded with either 3-prong plugs or pigtail adapters?					
57. Are electrical cords in good repair?					
58. Are service cords long enough so that extension cords are not needed?					
59. Are all electrical outlets in good repair?					

SAFETY SELF-INSPECTION FORM

AREA: Food Preparation Areas INSPECTED BY: DATE:

QUESTION	YES	NO	PROBLEM NOTED	CORRECTIONS	WHEN DONE
60. Are electrical outlets not overloaded? Are they out of danger of being splashed?					
61. Are electrical switches in a place where the equipment cannot be turned on accidentally, but are accessible for quick shut-off in an emergency?					
62. Is equipment unplugged before cleaning?					
63. Are equipment handles pushed in so they do not hang over the range?					
64. Are knives stored in racks or sheaths?					
65. Are knives sharp and in good repair?					
66. Are knives being used safely?					
67. Are matches for gas equipment being stored in a metal box away from gas equipment?					
68. Is area free of grease buildup? Check stoves, fryers, hoods, filters, etc.					
69. Are all stainless steel bowls and mixer attachments in good repair and free of rust?					

SAFETY SELF-INSPECTION FORM

AREA: Food Preparation Areas | INSPECTED BY: | DATE:

QUESTION	YES	NO	PROBLEM NOTED	CORRECTIONS	WHEN DONE
70. Are hazardous chemicals kept separate from food?					
71. Are the shut-off valves for steam equipment in good working order?					

SAFETY SELF-INSPECTION FORM

AREA: Serving and Dining Areas | INSPECTED BY: | DATE:

QUESTION	YES	NO	PROBLEM NOTED	CORRECTIONS	WHEN DONE
72. Are floors and walls in safe condition: dry, clean, no tiles missing or broken, no worn areas?					
73. Are ''Wet Floor'' signs available and used when needed?					
74. Is all lighting in working order and adequate?					
75. Are tables, counters, and equipment free from sharp corners and dangerous projections?					
76. Is ventilation sufficient?					
77. Are doors and aisles kept clear of supplies?					
78. Are there sufficient waste receptacles of leakproof, nonabsorbent material?					
79. Are waste receptacles covered?					
80. Are lids being lifted carefully to avoid steam burns?					
81. Do employees warn each other when carrying hot food?					

SAFETY SELF-INSPECTION FORM

AREA: Serving and Dining Areas INSPECTED BY: DATE:

QUESTION	YES	NO	PROBLEM NOTED	CORRECTIONS	WHEN DONE
82. Are chipped items of tableware being disposed of so they are not used to serve food?					
83. Are waitstaff trays not being overloaded?					
84. Are waitstaff trays being lifted with leg muscles rather than back muscles?					
85. Are tray stands in good repair and not blocking traffic?					
86. Are service doors marked for traffic flow, and are signs being observed?					
87. Are hazardous chemicals kept separate from food?					
88. Is all equipment working properly?					
89. Is equipment turned off when not in use?					
90. Is electrical equipment grounded with either 3-prong plugs or pigtail adapters?					
91. Are electrical cords in good repair?					

SAFETY SELF-INSPECTION FORM

AREA: Serving and Dining Area   INSPECTED BY: DATE:

QUESTION	YES	NO	PROBLEM NOTED	CORRECTIONS	WHEN DONE
92. Are service cords long enough so extension cords are not needed?					
93. Are all electrical outlets in good repair?					
94. Is equipment unplugged before cleaning?					

SAFETY SELF-INSPECTION FORM

AREA: Ware washing Areas INSPECTED BY: DATE:

QUESTION	YES	NO	PROBLEM NOTED	CORRECTIONS	WHEN DONE
95. Are floors and walls in safe condition: dry, clean, no tiles missing or broken, no worn areas?					
96. Are ''Wet Floor'' signs available and used when needed?					
97. Is all lighting in working order and adequate?					
98. Are tables, counters, and equipment free from sharp corners and dangerous projections?					
99. Is ventilation sufficient?					
100. Are doors and aisles kept clear of supplies?					
101. Are there sufficient waste receptacles of leakproof, nonabsorbent material?					
102. Are waste receptacles covered?					
103. Is there enough aisle space to prevent accidents?					
104. Are floors that stay wet covered with floor mats?					

SAFETY SELF-INSPECTION FORM

AREA: Ware washing Areas INSPECTED BY: DATE:

QUESTION	YES	NO	PROBLEM NOTED	CORRECTIONS	WHEN DONE
105. Are broken dishes and glasses being swept up promptly and disposed of per policy?					
106. Are employees trained on using chemicals safely?					
107. Are employees handling chemicals safely?					
108. Is there adequate space for air drying of equipment?					
109. Are gloves available?					
110. Are racks of dishes stacked neatly?					

SAFETY SELF-INSPECTION FORM

AREA: Waste Disposal Area INSPECTED BY: DATE:

QUESTION	YES	NO	PROBLEM NOTED	CORRECTIONS	WHEN DONE
111. Is the area clean and clear of debris such as broken glass and cans?					
112. Are floors and walls in safe condition: dry, clean, no tiles missing or broken, no worn areas?					
113. Are ''Wet Floor'' signs available and used when needed?					
114. Is all lighting in working order and adequate?					
115. Are tables, counters, and equipment free from sharp corners and dangerous projections?					
116. Is ventilation sufficient?					
117. Are employees instructed on how to use trash compaction devices?					
118. Do employees operate trash compactors safely?					
119. Are gloves available and being used?					
120. Is smoking forbidden in this area, and is this posted?					

SAFETY SELF-INSPECTION FORM

AREA: Hazardous Material Storage | INSPECTED BY: | DATE:

QUESTION	YES	NO	PROBLEM NOTED	CORRECTIONS	WHEN DONE
121. Are MSDSs (Material Safety Data Sheets) available to employees?					
122. Are hazardous materials being used according to instructions on MSDSs?					
123. Are flammable hazardous materials being stored in a safe manner?					
124. Are CO_2 tanks for soft drink machines protected from falling over?					
125. Do hazardous materials have identifying labels with instructions on how to use?					

SAFETY SELF-INSPECTION FORM

AREA: Employee Facilities INSPECTED BY: DATE:

QUESTION	YES	NO	PROBLEM NOTED	CORRECTIONS	WHEN DONE
126. Are floors and walls in safe condition: dry, clean, no tiles missing or broken, no worn areas?					
127. Is all lighting in working order and adequate?					
128. Is ventilation sufficient?					
129. Are doors and aisles kept clear of supplies?					
130. Are there sufficient waste receptacles of leakproof, nonabsorbent material?					
131. Are waste receptacles covered?					
132. Is equipment safe and in good repair?					
133. Are there safe receptacles for cigareetes?					

SAFETY SELF-INSPECTION FORM

AREA: Employees INSPECTED BY: DATE:

QUESTION	YES	NO	PROBLEM NOTED	CORRECTIONS	WHEN DONE
134. Do employees wear nonabsorbent shoes with nonskid soles and low heels? Nonskid soles may be made of rubber or neoprene.					
135. Do employees walk, not run?					
136. Are employees paying attention to what they are doing?					
137. Are employees wearing clothing and jewelry that will *not* get caught in equipment?					

SAFETY SELF-INSPECTION FORM

AREA: General   INSPECTED BY: DATE:

QUESTION	YES	NO	PROBLEM NOTED	CORRECTIONS	WHEN DONE
138. Are fire extinguishers visible and accessible?					
139. Are fire extinguishers inspected regularly?					
140. Do employees know where to find and how to use fire extinguishers?					
141. Are fats, oils, and matches stored in closed containers away from heat?					
142. Are ceiling sprinkler systems clear of obstacles?					
143. Are exits clearly marked and accessible?					
144. Do employees know what to do in case of a fire?					
145. Do stairs have adequate lighting?					
146. Are stairways clear of obstacles?					
147. Are electrical panels accessible and labeled?					

SAFETY SELF-INSPECTION FORM

AREA: General INSPECTED BY: DATE:

QUESTION	YES	NO	PROBLEM NOTED	CORRECTIONS	WHEN DONE
148. Are all hot pipes insulated?					
149. Are carts and trucks in good repair?					
150. Are no smoking rules being observed?					
151. Is ice-making equipment protected from foreign objects falling accidentally into the ice?					
152. Is there a scoop available for the ice machine and is it used?					
153. Is there a fully stocked first aid kit available?					
154. Do employees know where the first aid kit is?					
155. Are emergency phone numbers posted on or by the phone?					

INDEX